Senseless Panic

How Washington Failed America

William M. Isaac
with Philip C. Meyer

WILEY

John Wiley & Sons, Inc.

Published by John Wiley & Sons, Inc., Hoboken, New Jersey.
Published simultaneously in Canada.

For general information on our other products and services or for technical support, please contact our Customer Care Department within the United States at (800) 762-2974, outside the United States at (317) 572-3993 or fax (317) 572-4002.

Wiley also publishes its books in a variety of electronic formats. Some content that appears in print may not be available in electronic books. For more information about Wiley products, visit our web site at www.wiley.com.

Library of Congress Cataloging-in-Publication Data:

Isaac, William M., 1943-
    Senseless panic : how Washington failed America / William M. Isaac.
      p.   cm.
    Includes index.
    ISBN 978-0-470-64036-4 (cloth); ISBN 978-1-118-43198-6 (paper);
    ISBN 978-1-118-47319-1 (ebk); ISBN 978-1-118-47328-3 (ebk);
    ISBN 978-1-118-47332-0 (ebk)
      1. Savings and loan association failures—United States—History.   2. Savings and Loan Bailout, 1989-1995.   3. Global Financial Crisis, 2008-2009.   4. Bank failures—United States—History.   I. Title.
    HG2152.I88 2010
    332.10973—dc22

                                                                    2010008413

Printed in the United States of America

10 9 8 7 6 5 4 3 2

Senseless Panic

7/25/14

I dedicate this book to my family—the most important people in my life—and to the professional staff of the bank regulatory agencies, particularly the staff of the Federal Deposit Insurance Corporation, who are among the most dedicated and hardworking public servants I have known.

Contents

CONTENTS

Foreword

As you read *Senseless Panic* you can expect to be caught up in a financial saga. The story of that saga raises critical questions demanding an urgent response for the future of our banking system and more broadly for the capacity of our government to respond to crises. You will also quickly come to understand that Bill Isaac deserves to be listened to. Beyond his deep experience, he is a man of strong convictions, decisive in thought and courageous in action.

Those are not qualities that most Americans these days associate with men or women administering the work of the federal government. They were not qualities that, for many years, loomed large or necessary in choosing the board of the Federal Deposit Insurance Corporation.

The FDIC was created in 1933 in the wake of the banking collapse in the Great Depression. Its purpose was clear: to insure prompt payment in full for small deposits at failed banks. Combined with authority to examine thousands of banks, confidence in a shattered financial system could then be restored.

That was, and remains, an important purpose. For a while, however, the FDIC did not seem needed. The experience of the Depression induced bankers to be ultra-cautious. During and after World War II, the resurgent economy meant clear weather for banks. For decades, there were practically no bank failures, and the FDIC receded into a kind of bureaucratic backwater. It was not really challenged or influential in policy. When questions of regulatory practice arose, it was the Treasury or the Federal Reserve that held sway.

My first contact with the FDIC in 1963 perfectly reflected both the institutional hierarchy and the absence of challenge. The FDIC had just built a new building placed across 17th Street from the White House. Despite the location and the fine architecture, the opening was not a major Washington event. As a junior Treasury official, I was delegated to represent the department at the dedication ceremony. The speaker was the chairman of the House Banking Committee, one Wright Patman, a man engrained in the strong populist traditions of rural Texas. His theme was clear. There simply were not enough bank failures. The creative instincts of small business were stifled by conservative loan policies. The FDIC was simply doing its job too well.

Chairman Patman had long since left from Washington when his wish was amply fulfilled. A young Bill Isaac was appointed a FDIC board member in 1978, a year or so before the institution had to deal with the potential failure of a large (by the standards of 1970s) Philadelphia bank. The decision was made, with the Federal Reserve in the lead, to provide enough emergency assistance to keep the bank running. Bill Isaac was prescient in his concern that the approach could lead to a policy that some banks were simply "too big to fail."

Soon, Bill became chairman. It wasn't long before he and his agency were thrust into a decade-long succession of really serious threats to the stability of our depository institutions and to the U.S. economy. It started with the savings bank and agricultural bank crises, soon followed by the Latin American debt crisis, embroiling the largest international banks. The debacle of the deregulated savings and loan industry followed. One of the largest commercial banks—Continental Illinois—was rescued by the combined efforts of the FDIC and the Federal Reserve. There was a string of bank failures, and near failures, toward the end of the 1980s. The FDIC, along with the Federal Savings and Loan Insurance Corporation, the Federal Reserve, and the United States Treasury were together faced with unique challenges.

Senseless Panic is in part the story of that decade—the actions taken and the lessons learned and the lessons forgotten. The face of banking in the United States changed, with reverberations lasting to this day.

I was the chairman of the Federal Reserve in those days. Like my predecessors, I thought "the Fed" had a special role and broad responsibility for defending and maintaining financial stability. Truth be told, given the pattern over decades, we tended to look to the FDIC as a sort of junior partner. That, I think is fair to say, was *not* Bill Isaac's view—not when it came to failing banks.

My first impression of Bill was of a rather brash young man, certainly vigorous and self-assured, but perhaps lacking the seasoning that one might expect of an agency head. He was certainly not deferential. But as we got into the trenches together, I came to realize the importance of his character, of the personal strength desperately needed in perilous times.

Given all of that, there can be no surprise that Bill Isaac has strong views about the official response to the latest and most serious financial crisis. He sets out his view of the way ahead. There is no mincing of words. *Senseless Panic* is a clarion call to action by Congress, by the regulatory agencies, by accounting standards setters, by rating agencies, and by banks themselves.

I and others might challenge one or another of the specifics or relative priorities. But there can be no question that his sense of urgency is justified and his proposed policies need a thoughtful response.

There is another lesson to be drawn from this book. It concerns an issue never explicitly stated, but relevant and timely when there is such distrust of government and those who serve it.

Bill Isaac was a public servant. In a real sense, he still is, even if not now in formal office. What he demonstrated is that, by force of character and innate ability, he could arouse a rather forgotten old-line government agency into an active vital force, able to respond to crises with vigor and effectiveness.

Fortunately, that spirit remains in the leadership and staff of the FDIC today. It is dealing effectively with matters of momentous importance.

Bill's book amply reflects the sense of frustration, the exceptional demands emotionally and professionally placed on top officials and staff alike at times of crisis, the rigidity of bureaucracy, and the limitations on resources that are the lot of public servants. But what comes through it all is something else. It is the sense of pride, of having been tested to the maximum, of serving not a personal or a private interest but the American public.

Those are qualities that somehow we as a nation have been losing—not entirely, and I trust not permanently. Of one thing I am sure. We should not and cannot settle for less than a fair share of our country's best talent when manning the ramparts of governments. That is one key lesson of Bill Isaac's life story, a lesson at least as important as the reality of the banking crisis.

Paul A. Volcker
February 2010

Acknowledgments

I am grateful to Paul Volcker, Steve Forbes, Phil Meyer, Meg Maguire, Christie Sciacca, Bill Donaldson, Doug Marcian, Jack Ryan, Phil Zweig, Art Laffer, Marcy Kaptur, Jack Murphy, Ralph Nader, Larry Kudlow, Darrell Issa, Theron Raines, Alan Michaels, Peter Tanous, Gary Stern, Charles Isaac and many others who will remain unnamed for generously offering their comments about the book. They made the book better. The views expressed in this book are mine and are not necessarily shared by any of the above individuals or any organizations with which I am affiliated.

Special thanks to my wife, Christine, who encouraged me to battle against the TARP legislation and to write this book. She gave me unwavering support throughout the long hours I have devoted to this book and public policy issues over the past two years.

William M. Isaac
Sarasota, Florida
January 15, 2010

Introduction

The financial panic of 2008 and the ensuing deep recession did not have to happen, and I am appalled by the enormous financial, human, and political cost of it all. Taxpayers, rightly so, are extremely angry about the events of 2008 and 2009—they know instinctively that something does not smell right.

I wrote this book to get the truth out about what happened and why and how we can prevent future crises. We—and I mean all of us and our great country—are in enormous trouble! If we do not take the time to learn what went wrong and how to fix it, we and our children and their children will pay a very big price.

If we let them, our political leaders will do everything in their power to hide their culpability for the mess in which our nation finds itself, and they will enact politically easy legislation that will not address the fundamental causes of the crisis and will, in fact, make things worse. Our leaders are already covering up their role in creating what I call the Senseless Panic of 2008, are trying to deflect blame to "greedy bankers," and are offering slogans rather than solutions.

Among other things, they are telling us the Troubled Asset Relief Program (TARP) was essential to calming the markets when, in fact, the TARP did far more harm than good. This book exposes the TARP for what it was—an ill-conceived program hastily slapped together by a panicked government working too close for my comfort with a handful of Wall Street firms. It set off an economic and political firestorm from which we have yet to recover.

■■■

I had the privilege of leading the Federal Deposit Insurance Corporation during the bank and thrift crises of the 1980s, having been appointed to the FDIC board of directors by President Jimmy Carter in 1978 at the age of 34.

Little did I know when I took the post that the country was about to experience the worst economic and banking crisis since the Great Depression—a crisis that would result in larger and more severe bank failures than in the 1930s.

Inflation had been high throughout the 1970s and it was getting worse. President Carter appointed Paul Volcker as chairman of the Federal Reserve in 1979 with the charge of getting inflation under control. Volcker raised interest rates rapidly and the prime rate soared to an incredible 21.5 percent. Few financial institutions or borrowers could absorb that kind of rate increase.

Following Ronald Reagan's election in 1980, I was named chairman of the FDIC. The entire banking and thrift sector was in dire straits. A short recession occurred in 1980, followed by a deep and prolonged recession in 1981–1982, with unemployment soaring to almost 11 percent.

From 1980 through 1991, some 3,000 banks and thrifts failed, including many of the largest in the country (nine of the 10 largest Texas banks, for example). The failed banks and thrifts had

$650 billion of assets and cost the FDIC fund more than $100 billion (multiply those numbers by six to put them into relative terms to today's banking system).

It was an extremely difficult period, but the public's confidence in the banking system held and financial panic was averted. Even as we handled thousands of bank and thrift failures, the economy improved and we enjoyed the longest peacetime economic expansion in history.

Contrast this result in the 1980s with the worldwide financial panic that hit in the fall of 2008 and threatened to push the world into an economic depression. The economy was actually quite strong in pre-financial crisis 2007, unlike 1980–1982, so why did we experience such different outcomes in the financial markets?

It is impossible to listen to or read a news report about the crisis of 2008 and beyond without being told that the problems in this latest crisis are much worse than in any period since the Great Depression of the 1930s. When people do talk about the 1980s, most refer only to the S&L crisis and seem not to be aware how serious the banking and economic problems were during that period.

Most people—members of Congress included—would be surprised to learn that we were so concerned about the condition of our major banks during the 1980s that we developed a contingency plan to nationalize all of them. As late as the presidential debate of 1992, candidate Ross Perot asserted that the FDIC fund was horribly inadequate to cope with what he believed was the massive insolvency of our major banks.

■■■

In this book, I discuss how we were able to navigate the treacherous economic and banking waters in the 1980s without creating a financial panic and why we failed to contain the less serious problems in 2008 that nearly sank the financial system.

Having lived 24/7 with the banking and S&L crises of the 1980s, I examine the lessons we learned and failed to learn from that period and identify the mistakes that led to the Senseless Panic of 2008. It was a panic that would not have happened had our political leaders acquired even passing knowledge of what happened during the 1980s and how we dealt with the enormous problems.

Many historians believe that World War II was a continuation of World War I. They believe that the issues that led to the first war were not resolved and the Treaty of Versailles was terribly flawed, so after a 20-year hiatus, the fight was resumed.

Similarly, I believe the banking and S&L crises of the 1980s were misunderstood by our political leaders, the wrong fixes were put into place during the 1990s, and those actions led us directly into the banking crisis of 2008.

Based on what I have seen thus far from the Obama Administration and the legislative efforts on Capitol Hill, we have not gotten any smarter this time around and I fear for the future of our great nation.

Part One

NO CALM BEFORE THE STORM

Chapter 1

Home Alone

I was home alone in Sarasota, Florida, enjoying the tranquil waters of the Gulf of Mexico lapping against the shore. Saturday, September 27, 2008, was a typical steamy day toward the end of an uneventful hurricane season. A storm of another sort was brewing, however, and I was jolted back into reality by the loud ring of my landline. It was the first of many urgent calls I would receive that day from Washington, D.C.

In contrast to the Gulf of Mexico, the worldwide financial system was anything but tranquil. It was, in fact, in the midst of a veritable tsunami in the wake of the government's decision to allow the venerable investment bank of Lehman Brothers to fail on September 15.

On Thursday, September 18, Secretary of the Treasury Henry Paulson and Federal Reserve chairman Ben Bernanke rushed to Capitol Hill to meet with leaders of Congress in House Speaker Nancy Pelosi's conference room.

3

Paulson and Bernanke presented an outline of a $700 billion financial bailout plan, called "TARP," as in Troubled Asset Relief Program. The idea was for taxpayers to purchase $700 billion of bad assets from financial institutions. Their presentation was, in a word, terrifying.

"If we don't do this," Bernanke was reported as saying, "we may not have an economy on Monday."

Paulson used inflammatory terms like "financial Armageddon" to stress the need for urgent action.

Having served as chairman of the Federal Deposit Insurance Corporation (FDIC) during the banking and S&L crises of the 1980s, I was disturbed, even angry, about the events that led up to the bailout plan and the plan itself. I was so upset that I wrote an opinion piece opposing the bailout plan that ran in the *Washington Post* of Saturday, September 27.

My op-ed suggested a four-step plan to alleviate the financial crisis:

1. The Securities and Exchange Commission immediately reimpose on short sellers the Depression-era regulations on speculative abuses the SEC had removed in 2007
2. The FDIC declare a financial emergency and proclaim that all depositors and other creditors of banks would be protected in bank failures during the period of emergency
3. The SEC immediately suspend the mark-to-market accounting rules adopted by the SEC and the Financial Accounting Standards Board during the preceding decade (rules that senselessly destroyed over $500 billion of capital in our financial system)
4. The FDIC use its emergency power to restore capital in banks along the lines of a program we used successfully in the 1980s

I believed then and continue to believe strongly that these actions would have been much more effective in dampening the financial crisis than Paulson's ill-conceived plan to purchase toxic assets, would have cost taxpayers little, if any, money, and would not have politicized the crisis and scared the public the way the Paulson plan did.

The *Washington Post* article triggered a series of Saturday phone calls from members of Congress, urging me to come to Washington immediately to discuss the crisis and the bailout legislation. The calls were from three Democrats (Marcy Kaptur of Ohio, Brad Sherman of California, and John Hall of New York) and two Republicans (Darrell Issa of California and Vern Buchanan of Florida).

Not only were they from different parties, they represented a pretty broad swath of the political spectrum. They had in common fears about the financial system, deep skepticism about Paulson's bailout plan, and frustration that the congressional leadership was rushing headlong into adopting the bailout plan without hearings, debate, or amendments.

I knew Marcy Kaptur, as she was on the House Banking Committee when I served as chairman of the FDIC, and she is from Toledo, Ohio, near my hometown of Bryan, Ohio. Vern Buchanan is my congressman in Sarasota. I had not met the others but would soon get to know them pretty well.

To this day, I do not know if their calls were coordinated or independent of one another, but my sense is that they were independent. I told each that I could see no point in coming.

"Congress is going to approve the bailout bill on Monday," I explained, "and my presence in Washington is not going to change anything. We are taking the kids to see the Buccaneers play the Packers tomorrow and that's a much better way for me to spend my weekend."

Several persisted. Brad Sherman offered to pay my expenses, but I declined. I teased John Hall, a former rock musician who founded the group Orleans, that my price for coming would be an invitation to watch his current group perform. He has yet to deliver, but I will remind him some day.

"Okay," I finally said. "When my wife gets home, I will ask her what she thinks."

When she returned, her response was immediate and unwavering, "You have to go. You feel so strongly about these things, you will always regret it if you don't."

She was right. The next day, my wife and kids went to the Bucs game without me and I took off for Washington. I went because I was convinced that our leaders had failed us for the last two decades, and because I hoped that I might be able to help prevent a bad situation from becoming even worse by tapping the lessons of the bank and savings and loan crises of the 1980s.

I could not have guessed how much my life would change. I have devoted at least half of my time since September 28, 2008, to trying to help get us out of this crisis and make sure we do not ever experience another one.

■■■

My flight from nearby Tampa landed at Reagan National in Washington at one o'clock in the afternoon on Sunday, September 28, and a waiting Lincoln Town Car whisked me directly to Capitol Hill. The next few days were a whirlwind.

Congressman Issa generously offered his office as a staging area. His staff put out the word to Republicans and Democrats alike that I was available to meet with any member of Congress who wanted to discuss the financial crisis or the bailout legislation.

There were plenty of takers. I had a series of meetings of various sizes with members of Congress that lasted until one o'clock Monday morning, when I finally checked into my hotel and crashed for a few hours. Most of the meetings were conducted in windowless rooms that I never knew existed in the basement of the Capitol Building.

All together, I met with some 200 members of Congress from both parties from the left, right, and middle of the political spectrum. Several of the meetings were joint meetings of Republicans and Democrats, which participants told me they had never witnessed previously.

I will never forget one meeting in particular. Congressman Jesse Jackson (D-Ill.) was on my left, Congressman Dennis Kucinich (D-Ohio) was on my right, and Congresswoman Maxine Waters (D-Calif.) was directly across the table with a number of conservative Republicans sprinkled around the rectangular table. I was thrilled to see them set aside partisanship and ideology for a moment and come together for the good of the country.

For the most part, the meetings were with the rank and file members of the two parties, not the leadership. The leaders of both parties had already made up their minds that the Paulson bill should be adopted immediately without hearings, debate, or significant changes. The leadership viewed the skeptics as an annoyance. As if to put an exclamation point on it, the floor vote in the House was scheduled for Monday morning, September 29.

As the day turned to evening on Sunday, the leadership began to realize that it had a rebellion on its hands. At the urging of the skeptics, the Republican leadership group in the House granted me a half-hour to present my views. I was honored to be there and appreciated their willingness to listen and engage on the issues.

The Democratic Caucus, again at the urging of the rank and file, agreed to meet with Professor James Galbraith of the University of Texas and me later that evening, a most unusual step. Unfortunately, by the time we were allowed into the meeting, nearly all of the Democratic leaders had departed.

I returned to the Hill Monday morning to be available to any members who wanted to talk before the vote on the bill. We could not get a reading on when the vote would take place. We were given a time and then we were told it had been pushed back. It seemed the leadership was in trouble on the bill and was trying to round up votes.

Finally, definitive word was received that the vote would begin early in the afternoon. We fought a good fight, but evidently the leadership had mustered the needed votes. Otherwise, why take a vote?

I camped out in Darrell Issa's office to watch the vote on C-SPAN. It was every bit as exciting as a football game. The vote seesawed back and forth, the yeas and nays never more than a few votes apart. As the end drew near, the nays took a decisive lead and the bill was defeated—228 opposed and 205 in favor.

Cheers erupted throughout Darrell's office. We turned up the volume on the news channels to see how the news was being received. The world was as flabbergasted as we were!

The Dow Jones Industrial Average had been off significantly (in the range of negative 500 or more) most of the morning before the vote was taken and ended the day down over 700. A lot was made of that by critics of the House rejection, but I thought it represented a pretty subdued reaction for the market to drop another 200 points or so after the vote. The market rallied nearly 500 points the next day.

Congressman Buchanan and his wife, Sandy, and I rushed to Dulles Airport right after the vote to fly back to Sarasota. We were thrilled with the vote but knew the leadership was not going to let the vote stand.

■■■

Sure enough, the next day congressional leaders were working with the Bush Administration to sweeten the bill. A provision increasing the deposit insurance limit from $100,000 to $250,000 was added to buy support from smaller banks. Senator Chuck Schumer (D-N.Y.) called to ask if that amendment would move me to support the bill. I responded it would not.

About $150 billion of pork was added to buy more votes. Congressmen were threatened with the loss of committee memberships and support for their campaigns. Language was added requiring the SEC to provide a report on the effects of mark-to-market accounting. Moreover, the SEC announced a 30-day ban on short selling of financial stocks.

The Senate passed the bill by an overwhelming vote on Wednesday, October 1. I was particularly disappointed that Senator John McCain (R-Ariz.) came off the campaign trail to vote in favor of the bailout. I believe his vote was a nail in the coffin of his presidential campaign. If he had remained true to his core beliefs and voted against the horrendously bad Paulson bill, I believe he would have tapped into the very deep public anger toward Wall Street and Washington. One of my heroes was Senator Richard Shelby (R-Ala.), ranking member of the Senate Banking Committee. He railed against the Paulson bill on the White House lawn after a meeting in which President Bush asked for his support!

I returned to Washington the day of the Senate vote to be available to members of Congress prior to the House vote. The House voted narrowly in favor of the amended bill on Friday, October 3. The leadership prevailed, but at least some of what the skeptics had argued for had gotten into the legislation.

The Administration and congressional leaders made a huge deal about their belief that the markets were counting on passage of the TARP legislation, predicting that the Dow would drop at least 1,000 points if the bill were not passed. Once the bill did pass, the markets sobered up to the recognition that Congress just spent over $850 billion (counting the pork added to the TARP money) the Treasury did not have so it could pay for a bill that would do no good. The Dow dropped from 10,831 on October 1, 2008, to 8,175 on October 27, 2008. It continued its downward spiral to 6,547 on March 9, 2009. It is difficult to imagine how rejection of the bill could have produced worse results.

Each of the four actions I urged in the September 27 *Washington Post* op-ed piece was put into place after the TARP bill became law. The SEC adopted a temporary ban on short sales of financial stocks. The SEC also proposed to reinstitute a version of the short-sale regulations it had seen fit to abolish in 2007. Better late than never, unless, of course, you have already lost your house or your job, or your bank has failed and you cannot get a line of credit!

The SEC and FASB finally made significant reforms to mark-to-market accounting in early April 2009, but only after Congress held a scathing hearing in March 2009 (at which I testified) and threatened to legislate repeal of mark-to-market accounting if the SEC and FASB did not act immediately to correct its most egregious problems. The April action by the SEC and FASB was an improvement and was well received in the markets. But we really needed retroactive repeal of virtually all vestiges of mark-to-market accounting to restore much of the $500 billion of capital in our financial system that mark-to-market accounting had senselessly destroyed.

On October 14, less than two weeks after the TARP was enacted, Secretary Paulson announced that he was triggering the systemic risk exception to allow the FDIC to guarantee checking accounts and the debt of banks and bank holding companies. It was not the simple and reassuring blanket proclamation I had urged, but it had a similar effect.

Even more striking, Paulson aborted his plan to buy toxic loans under the Troubled Asset Relief Program in favor of using the money to recapitalize banks! I hate the way he got there and the way he implemented it, but he deep-sixed the Troubled Asset Relief Plan and decided to focus the money on recapitalizing the banks, as I had urged in the *Washington Post* article.

■■■

Twelve months later, when we observed the one-year anniversary of TARP, a fair number of political leaders credited TARP with calming the financial crisis—a lame defense at best. What else would we expect of people who gave $700 billion of our money to the Treasury secretary to distribute as he saw fit?

The irony is that while TARP was being considered, Barney Frank (D–Mass.), chairman of the House Financial Services Committee, when confronted by the skeptics about the plan I advocated in the *Washington Post* article, reportedly responded, "Isaac did a good job running the FDIC in the 1980s, but this crisis is much more complex due to all of the derivatives and other off-balance sheet exposures and requires different solutions. Isaac's experience is outdated."

Frank went on to draw an analogy to Joe Gibbs, who took the Washington Redskins to the Super Bowl several times during the 1980s and early 1990s but was unable to repeat when he coached the team more than a decade later. I was flattered to be compared to Joe Gibbs, but was not sure what to make of Barney's suggestion that I was over the hill, except to note that Barney is nearly four years older than I.

In fact, TARP accomplished nothing that could not have been done without legislation. The SEC could have suspended mark-to-market accounting and reinstituted regulations on short sellers without legislation. The FDIC could have guaranteed depositors and other creditors of banks without legislation. Moreover, the FDIC did not need legislation to develop a capital infusion program for banks under the systemic risk exception—had it done so, the program would have been administered far better and more fairly than the TARP program run by Treasury.

If we had gone down this path using the SEC's and FDIC's existing authority, we would not have forced Congress to appropriate taxpayer money with all of the harsh political consequences for both politicians and financial institutions. We would not have endured the political spectacle of our leaders using such inflammatory language as "financial Armageddon," "worst crisis since the Great Depression," and "not sure if we will even have a financial system on Monday."

The rhetoric used by political leaders to sell the TARP legislation seriously eroded public confidence in the government and the financial system and panicked the public. The economy flatlined during the month of October.

I will come back to all of this later, but first I will take you on a journey through the banking crisis of the 1980s through my eyes. I believe that understanding how we addressed the severe crisis of the 1980s is critical to understanding how we mishandled the problems of 2008.

Chapter 2

The Early Years (1978–1981)

George LeMaistre was chairman of the FDIC when I was appointed to the three-member board in 1978. More than twice my age and a very wise and kindly Southern gentleman, he took me under his wing and provided much-needed guidance to a 34-year-old from Bryan, Ohio.

My first day in office proved to be a precursor of things to come. The FDIC's corporate secretary, Alan Miller, flew to Louisville, where I was living, and administered my oath of office in the lobby of the Galt House Hotel in downtown along the banks of the Ohio River. We rushed to the airport to catch a flight to Puerto Rico to handle an $800 million bank failure (around $5 billion in today's terms), which was a big deal at the time. I discovered immediately that I had much to learn.

Inflation was out of control because of large oil price increases and years of undisciplined monetary, fiscal, and regulatory policies, so President Carter appointed Paul Volcker to be the chairman of the Federal Reserve Board. Paul and his colleagues at the Fed courageously tightened the money supply and the prime rate shot up to an astounding 21.5 percent.

One of the first banking casualties was First Pennsylvania Bank, the largest bank in Pennsylvania, which had invested heavily in long-term, fixed-rate government bonds. As interest rates soared, the value of the bank's bonds plummeted. The FDIC injected $325 million of capital into the bank in 1980 to prevent its failure.

The FDIC historically took its cue from the Fed and Treasury in its handling of major bank failures and this held true on the bailout of First Pennsylvania. I argued within the FDIC against bailing out First Pennsylvania and its management and directors from their mistakes and thought it would set a very bad precedent.

Most of the FDIC senior staff agreed with my view, but Irv Sprague, who had replaced George LeMaistre as chairman, had made up his mind to do the transaction. Sprague had spent most of his career as a political operative in Washington and was not about to rock the boat. Comptroller of the Currency John Heimann, the third member of the FDIC board, was fully supportive, because the Comptroller's office is part of the Treasury.

I struggled with it but decided not to cast a symbolic vote against the rescue package when it came before the FDIC board. I am torn about my vote to this day, even though it would not have made a difference. I decided that we should present a united front, but I felt like I compromised my principles.

Before the collapse of First Pennsylvania, bank and S&L regulators were not particularly focused on safety and soundness issues. We spent much of our time in interminable meetings discussing Community Reinvestment Act regulations, truth-in-lending enforcement, Home Mortgage Disclosure Act regulations, and other consumer protection measures enacted by Congress. Unfortunately, when times are good, regulators, Congress, and bankers tend to become complacent about bank safety and focus their attention elsewhere.

This was very much the case in the decade leading up to the crisis of 2008. Bank regulators during that period spent inordinate amounts of energy on compliance issues such as anti-money laundering enforcement, fair lending enforcement, the Community Reinvestment Act, and customer privacy. Of course, bankers need to put a good deal of their energy into whatever issues are of concern to their regulators and customers. I believe our nation would have been well served if bankers and regulators alike had kept their eye on the ball and devoted more energy to traditional safety and soundness issues.

"Safety and soundness has to be our highest priority," I told more than one consumer advocacy group during my chairmanship of the FDIC. "If we don't get that right, you won't have to worry about fair lending or any other kind of lending because there won't be any."

The collapse of First Pennsylvania in 1980 was a wake-up call. I met with Sprague to voice my concerns about other institutions that were vulnerable in a prolonged period of high interest rates. FDIC-insured mutual savings banks, with their portfolios of long-term, fixed-rate loans and bonds, were at the top of my list. These were institutions much like S&Ls with a concentrated presence in New York City and the Northeast generally. I was also worried about banking groups, such as the Butcher banks in Tennessee, which had borrowed heavily to finance acquisitions.

■■■

Sprague asked me to establish and chair an FDIC task force to determine the magnitude of the problems in the savings bank industry and develop a plan for handling them. The task force had representatives from the FDIC's legal, bank supervisory, research, and liquidation divisions.

We agreed on best case, worst case, and most likely case scenarios for future interest rates. Losses at each savings bank were projected under each interest rate scenario, and we estimated the number of months it would take each bank to deplete its capital. The FDIC's income from premiums and interest on its investment portfolio was projected under each scenario.

We decided that the maturity of the FDIC's portfolio of government bonds should be shortened significantly. While this would decrease the FDIC's income if interest rates declined, it would increase the income if interest rates remained at high levels. Since the number and cost of savings bank failures would climb in a high-rate environment, we believed the FDIC's investment strategy should hedge against this risk.

We debated how aggressive we should be in dealing with the savings banks. A lot of people believed the problems in the savings banks and the S&Ls (which were the responsibility of the now-defunct Federal Savings and Loan Insurance Corporation) were temporary because of the very high interest rates. They argued that as long as thrifts had the cash flow to meet their obligations, the government should not precipitate their demise. They urged the regulators to adopt new accounting rules to mask the condition of thrifts; relax capital requirements; allow weak institutions to merge with each other with the resulting accounting goodwill being added to their capital; and permit weak institutions to grow more rapidly to add newer, higher-yielding loans and investments.

This view of the problems and the appropriate solutions was nearly universal outside the confines of the FDIC. It was held by the Reagan Administration, the Federal Home Loan Bank Board and the FSLIC, nearly all state banking departments, most Congressional representatives, and the thrift industry trade groups.

Our task force rejected this approach. We believed the FDIC's minimum capital ratio of 5 percent should be enforced. Savings banks that fell below that level should be monitored closely and instructed that they could not bid up deposit interest rates, grow, or engage in risky activities.

We decided that if a savings bank's book capital fell below zero, it should be merged into a stronger bank with FDIC financial assistance. Both commercial banks and savings banks would be invited to bid, but we preferred to sell the failing bank to another savings bank. By selling a failing savings bank to another savings bank, we hoped to resolve two potential problems with one assistance package. The resulting entity, in any event, had to be viable and unlikely to fail.

We were not sure if the FDIC fund would be sufficient to handle all of the potential savings bank failures under the worst case scenario. We nonetheless believed that it was essential for us to craft real solutions to real problems. To do otherwise would only lead to more serious problems down the line.

Weak savings banks with nothing to lose would, if left to their own devices, take inordinate risks. Their desperation tactics would not only create additional losses for them, they would infect the climate for their competitors. Our first responsibility was to keep the problems contained. If we ran out of money to craft real solutions, we would ask Congress for more.

The really important point here is that we got out in front of the looming savings bank crisis. The FDIC spent months tapping the best minds it could find inside and outside the agency and developing a coherent strategy for handling the savings bank problems. The months of planning and the coherent strategy paid big dividends when the problems hit us full blast in 1981.

In contrast, I saw precious little evidence that the government even recognized in 2007 that a significant downturn was a possibility, much less devoted any significant effort to developing a strategy for dealing with it. As far as I can tell, we were caught with our collective pants down.

■ ■ ■

I had not planned to serve my full six-year term on the FDIC board. Serving as a minority board member might be a fascinating experience, but not one likely to hold my interest beyond a couple of years. My plans changed when Ronald Reagan defeated Jimmy Carter in the 1980 election.

The Reaganites, suspicious of anyone who had not worked on behalf of Ronald Reagan's election, given their preference, would have appointed someone other than me as chairman. Fortunately or unfortunately, depending on your point of view, because of our fixed terms they had to either keep Sprague as chairman or elevate me. They decided I was the lesser evil, and I was named chairman in 1981. Todd Conover was appointed Comptroller of the Currency, becoming an ex officio member of the FDIC board.

I was grateful I had been on the FDIC board for three years before becoming chairman. It gave me an opportunity to get to know the agency and its people and to understand the environment. I had no idea how bad the banking crisis would get, but I was certain the savings bank problems alone would pose the most severe test in FDIC history. I was not sure that either the FDIC's staff or I was up to the challenge.

The FDIC's only experience in dealing with sizable bank failures (apart from First Pennsylvania, which had not been allowed to actually fail) had been in 1973 and 1974 when U.S. National Bank in San Diego and Franklin National Bank in New York went under. The savings bank problems were far greater in number and size. Moreover, no one in a senior position at the FDIC in 1981 had any significant involvement with the failures of U.S. National or Franklin.

I believed we needed to organize the agency to deal more effectively with the coming onslaught. We consolidated a lot of functions, reducing the number of people reporting to the chairman from thirteen to six.

I designated those six people as the FDIC's Management Committee. The management committee met for lunch weekly and had quarterly offsite meetings to focus on strategic issues and long-range planning.

I took these steps, which proved successful, for several reasons. The FDIC had done almost no forward planning, and we could no longer afford to be so casual. The FDIC had been a very turf-conscious agency, with the heads of the various divisions and offices seldom communicating and cooperating the way they would need to if we were to meet the challenges ahead. The problems facing us were complex and the stakes enormous, so I felt we needed to bring together our most experienced people and institute a consensus-based decision-making process.

To encourage greater understanding and cooperation, we decided to rotate division heads and senior deputies from time to time. Moreover, we instituted the FDIC's first management development program. Each year, several bright young stars were selected to enter the program. They were rotated through responsible positions throughout the agency and given the opportunity to participate in executive education programs at Harvard, Wharton, and other graduate schools. One of my great pleasures looking back years later was to see that a large proportion of the agency's next generation of leaders had come through the management development program.

The management committee decided early on that we needed to redirect the agency and its staff. The FDIC was established to insure bank deposits and resolve failures in an orderly way. After the agency handled a bunch of small bank failures during its early years, its insurance and liquidation functions received scant attention.

The agency focused most of its attention on regulating, in conjunction with state banking departments, thousands of state banks that were not members of the Federal Reserve System. While these banks constituted some two-thirds of the nation's banks, they were small and held only a third of the banking assets.

■■■

So the agency our country was depending on to identify and resolve significant banking problems did not have the means to do so. Our people were located in relatively small cities supervising relatively small banks. The FDIC had no knowledge of what was going on in the large banks that posed the greatest threats to the FDIC fund. Getting talented personnel relocated to large cities and training them to deal with larger banks was vitally important.

To do that, we had to address the compensation system. The FDIC, as an independent agency, was not legally bound to follow government pay scales but it had always done so. A grade 15 government employee located in Racine, Wisconsin, was paid the same amount as a grade 15 located in New York City. To induce people to relocate to large cities, we adopted a liberal program to cover all the costs of the move, and we instituted a regional pay differential to provide more compensation to employees in higher-cost cities. We also established a bonus program to reward senior people who performed ably in difficult circumstances. To keep turnover as low as possible, we enhanced significantly the FDIC's benefit programs to make the agency the best employer in the government.

By the time we were done, some 75 employees of the FDIC made more than I, as my compensation was set by law. My predecessor, Irv Sprague, who remained on the board, argued against the "glittering array of benefit programs." He said other agencies would complain, and Congress would respond by curtailing the FDIC's independence. I believed it was a risk we had to take.

I said to Sprague, "What's the point of having independence if we don't use it?"

A few years after I left the FDIC, Congress did learn of the FDIC's innovations and enacted legislation to permit other financial regulators to offer the same programs.

While the carrots we offered were pretty effective in getting the right people to move to the right locations, we needed to find a way to bring about a larger-scale reorientation of the FDIC's resources. We phased out six of the FDIC's 12 regional offices, closing those in smaller cities. We froze hiring in the regions the Division of Bank Supervision believed were over-staffed with examiners focused on small banks. Regions that had larger or troubled banks, such as Dallas and San Francisco, were allowed to hire as many examiners as they could train.

■ ■ ■

I viewed the FDIC as a sleeping giant. It had a broad charter, an exceptionally dedicated staff, and enormous financial resources. The agency had not been called upon to live up to its full potential since its creation some 50 years earlier. On those few occasions it had been called into action, such as the failures of Franklin National and First Pennsylvania, it generally took its cue from the Treasury and the Federal Reserve.

With the savings bank and other problems looming, it was time to wake up the agency. We did not know just how bad the crisis would be, but we knew it would almost certainly be the most challenging undertaking in the FDIC's history. I hoped the agency and I were ready for what was to come.

Chapter 3

The Savings Bank and S&L Crises

The savings bank crisis hit hard in the fall of 1981. Greenwich Savings Bank, a $3 billion institution in New York City, was on the brink of failure. To put this in context, a $3 billion bank in 1981 is roughly equivalent to a $20 billion bank in 2008 in terms of relative size within the banking system.

We invited other banks to a bidders' conference to arrange an FDIC-assisted merger for the bank. Because there was insufficient space to hold the meeting at the FDIC's New York office, we decided to hold the meeting in a private room at the Vista Hotel. That proved to be a very big mistake.

Laura Gross, an enterprising young reporter for the *American Banker*, used her impressive sleuthing skills to find out when and where the meeting was being held. She called a lot of senior people at the FDIC only to be told that they were "out of town" or "at a conference." Finally, an FDIC secretary volunteered that an official was "in New York City." Laura called every hotel in New York City until she found the one in which the official was staying—the Vista Hotel in the World Trade Center. She found the meeting room the FDIC had reserved and stationed herself, looking very official with a clipboard in hand, at the elevators on the appropriate floor. As bankers got off the elevators she asked if they were there for the FDIC meeting, took down their names, and directed them to the proper room.

The next day she ran a front-page story reporting on the FDIC's little party. The general media picked up the story, and we had an old-fashioned bank run on our hands. We accelerated our bidding schedule on Greenwich, as the bank lost some $500 million in deposits in just a couple of days.

The new chairman of the FDIC was not off to a flying start. I was more than a little annoyed with Laura, but had to admire her tenacity and ingenuity. Needless to say, we never held another bidders' meeting outside government offices.

■■■

While the Greenwich episode was not pleasant at the time, it offered some valuable lessons. It brought home the seriousness of the problems we were facing. A lot of large savings banks were in big trouble. Their depositors tended to be older people with memories of the Great Depression. They were very nervous and were not sure whether and how the FDIC would protect their savings. We would be watched carefully every step of the way.

This led me to reconsider the FDIC's long-standing practice of avoiding the media. When Sprague hired Alan Whitney as director of corporate communications, he told Alan that if he saw his or the FDIC's name in the press, Alan should consider that to be a failure.

The public can handle almost any information, no matter how bad. What the public cannot handle is misinformation or no information. We adopted a policy of openness and candor—the buzzword today is "transparency," which I dislike because it is so overused.

At the beginning of each year during my tenure, we met with the press to provide an estimate of how many banks would fail during the year. We reasoned that if we were expecting a large number of failures, it would be better to tell the public we were expecting them and were prepared to deal with them than to just let them happen unannounced. While the specific banks could not be predicted with precision, our estimates of total failures each year proved uncannily accurate.

The openness policy served us well. Not long after I joined the FDIC, I had a discussion with some of the FDIC's old hands, speculating on how many bank failures the public could handle in a given year without creating a panic. The consensus was that 25 to 30 small banks would be the limit of the public's tolerance. The FDIC handled 120 large and small bank failures during my last year as chairman and the annual total rose to as high as 200 failures after I left (and much higher than that after Congress gave the FDIC responsibility in 1989 for resolving S&L failures). The public was calm once it became clear the FDIC was on top of things.

As I watched the crisis of 2008 unfold, I was distressed to see the apparent lack of a coherent strategy for getting in front of the problems rather than slapping together ad hoc solutions for each problem as it surfaced. I was equally concerned about the lack of straight talk about what was happening and how the government planned to deal with it.

Despite our stumbling start at Greenwich Savings Bank, the resolution of the savings bank crisis stands as one of the FDIC's finest accomplishments. The work of the savings bank task force served us well and the policies it recommended were implemented. The projections of which savings banks would fail, and when, were right on target.

The FDIC's handling of the savings bank crisis was enormously unpopular in industry and political circles. We were under tremendous pressure to follow the course set by the FSLIC for the S&L industry. We were urged to turn our backs on the problems, to help hide them, and to allow the savings banks to grow out of them.

Congressional hearings criticized the FDIC's harsh treatment of the savings banks. Congress passed a law in 1982 requiring the FDIC to grant forbearance to savings banks through a "net worth certificate" program, aimed at strengthening the capital of savings banks through FDIC infusions of capital. We implemented the program, but we did not fundamentally alter our approach toward the savings banks. We would allow only banks we judged to be viable with help from the program to enter the program, and we maintained tight control on their activities and growth.

At the height of the savings bank crisis, the industry was insolvent by more than $100 billion if its loans and investments were marked to market. Fortunately, and very unlike the circumstances nearly three decades later, we did not have to mark their assets to market and were able to work out the problems over time. When all was said and done, the FDIC resolved the crisis for just under $2 billion.

The S&L industry faced similar problems of comparable magnitude. When all was said and done, the FSLIC was rendered insolvent and U.S. taxpayers were required to fork over nearly $150 billion.

The big difference was that the FDIC confronted and contained the savings bank problems while the FSLIC obscured the S&L problems and allowed the cancer to spread. An interest rate mismatch problem in the S&L industry was allowed to become an asset quality problem of enormous dimensions.

■■■

I was deeply concerned about what we saw happening in the S&L industry. The problems at weak and insolvent firms were being masked. S&Ls were permitted to grow at inordinate rates with virtually no supervision. I was concerned this would infect not only them, but their bank and thrift competitors.

I called for a merger of the FSLIC into the FDIC. I argued that the FSLIC did not have the staff, the money, or the political will to deal with the S&L problems. This was one of my more unpopular suggestions.

The Federal Home Loan Bank Board viewed the idea as an attempt by the FDIC and me to grab power. The truth is that the FDIC staff already had its hands full and told me they thought it would be a mistake for the FDIC to take on the additional burden of resolving the S&L problems.

The S&L industry viewed the FDIC as an onerous and unsympathetic regulator to be avoided at all costs. Banks viewed as heresy my suggestion that their FDIC fund be used to help resolve the S&L problems. It was virtually impossible to find anybody inside or outside the FDIC who agreed with me, which was really frustrating because I felt certain that merging the two deposit insurance funds was the best way to keep the S&L problems from growing exponentially.

I asked the FDIC staff in 1984 to do a study to estimate the magnitude of the S&L problems and determine what it would take for the FDIC to resolve them. The study estimated that the FSLIC was insolvent to the tune of $15 billion.

President Reagan was reelected that fall, and James Baker was named Secretary of the Treasury. I met with Baker and gave him a copy of the FDIC's study. I told him the S&L problem was one of the most pressing financial issues confronting the nation. It would continue to escalate until addressed properly.

Allowing marginal S&Ls to pay high rates for deposits to fund high-risk loans wreaked havoc in the marketplace. Healthier banks and thrifts were under great pressure to follow suit. Much of the S&L industry was decimated. Commercial banks in areas where high-flying thrifts were most prevalent suffered grievous losses, costing the FDIC tens of billions of dollars.

■ ■ ■

Nothing of consequence was done until 1989 when George H. W. Bush was elected president. The first Bush Administration, to its credit, made the S&L crisis a top priority.

A problem that could have been resolved at a cost of $15 billion in 1984, without using taxpayer funds, escalated into a crisis that cost taxpayers nearly $150 billion (roughly equivalent to $450 billion today in terms of percentage of the total federal budget). One of my biggest disappointments is that I could not persuade people to recognize the severity of the S&L problems and deal with them much sooner.

Congress reacted to the taxpayer losses in the S&L industry by enacting a number of reforms that would come back to haunt us in 2008 and 2009. I will go into these reforms in more detail later, but one unfortunate reform was a law known as Prompt Corrective Action (PCA). PCA requires the regulators to take increasingly harsh actions (including closure) against banks as their capital falls below certain trigger points. If PCA had been in effect during the 1980s, the FDIC would have been forced to take enormously greater losses on the savings banks rather than putting them under tight controls while allowing them time to work through their problems.

It is true that the Federal Home Loan Bank Board and FSLIC allowed insolvent S&Ls to grow and increase their risks enormously. But that policy was strongly supported by the Reagan

Administration and the Congress. This was not the case of a lax or rogue regulator—the regulator was following policies handed down from on high.

I opposed Prompt Corrective Action (PCA) and wrote several articles predicting we would regret it when the next crisis hit. That time is now. PCA is forcing regulators to close banks that might otherwise be saved and is increasing resolution costs greatly by forcing more bank failures than necessary at the bottom of the cycle. Banks facing possible Prompt Corrective Action tend to sell their best-performing assets in an attempt to maintain their capital ratios above the trigger points for PCA. This leaves weaker institutions less capable of surviving. On top of that, PCA is grossly unfair to community banks, as they are dropping like flies while the largest banks have been declared too big to fail.

Chapter 4

Penn Square Fails

We were just hitting our stride with the savings banks when I got an urgent call from Paul Homan, senior deputy Comptroller of the Currency, a couple of days before the Fourth of July weekend in 1982. He needed to see me right away.

Homan sat in my office explaining that a $500 million national bank in an Oklahoma City shopping center was on the brink. I interrupted to ask why he was making such a big deal out of a small bank failure. It turns out the bank was the now-infamous Penn Square Bank.

Penn Square was a high-flying bank financing the speculative boom in the oil patch. While it was only $500 million in size (roughly $3 billion in today's terms), it had originated and was servicing some $3 billion of loans it had sold to major banks. The principal purchasers of these dubious loans were Chase

29

Manhattan, Continental Illinois, SeaFirst Bank, and Michigan National. If Penn Square were not handled properly, argued Homan, these much larger banks could suffer severe losses and might even fail.

Although I did not realize it at the time, the FDIC was about to come into its own. The next several days were filled with virtually around the clock negotiations and preparations. When I slept, it was on my office sofa.

Under the law at that time, if the FDIC arranged a merger for Penn Square and put FDIC money in the deal, all creditors of Penn Square, not just insured depositors, would need to be made whole. This would create two problems for the FDIC.

First, the large banks that purchased billions in bad loans would assert claims against Penn Square for negligence and fraud in originating and servicing the loans. If they proved their claims, they would be entitled to be made whole by the FDIC on the entire $3 billion. Our deposit insurance fund totaled roughly $11 billion so that was not a happy thought.

Second, there appeared to be a fair amount of fraud at Penn Square. If the FDIC arranged a merger for Penn Square, it would expose itself to the risk that it would be required to make whole creditors whose claims did not even appear on the financial statements of Penn Square.

So the FDIC was determined not to arrange a merger for Penn Square. The bank would be allowed to fail and the FDIC would pay the claims of insured depositors only.

The FDIC's position was not embraced warmly at the Federal Reserve or the Comptroller's office. They believed the FDIC should arrange a merger for Penn Square and make all creditors whole, whatever the cost. The debate grew more intense as the long Fourth of July weekend progressed.

Mike Bradfield, general counsel for the Federal Reserve (who is now general counsel of the FDIC), met with me in my office and insisted that the FDIC bail out Penn Square. I countered that the FDIC could not do that because we were governed by a statutory cost test that would not allow us to implement a resolution that was more expensive than a payoff of insured deposits with limited exceptions. Arranging a merger and assuming responsibility for billions of dollars of negligence and fraud claims at Penn Square would hardly qualify.

"Okay, Mike, I'll make you a deal," I finally said to Bradfield. "The FDIC will bail out Penn Square if the Fed will share half the cost of the bailout above the $250 million we estimate a straight failure of the bank will cost us."

"You know we can't do that," he retorted. "We don't have any legal authority."

"Neither do we," I replied. "If you want the FDIC to violate its cost test, then join us."

That brought the meeting to an abrupt end, but the debate was far from over. Top officials of the banks that bought loans from Penn Square met with the FDIC staff and me to argue for a bailout. Pressure was coming from all directions.

■■■

The FDIC could not close Penn Square. Only the bank's primary regulator, in this case the Comptroller, could do that and only after he found it was insolvent.

There are two types of insolvencies. The first is *book insolvency*—the value of a bank's assets is less than its liabilities. Because the problems at Penn Square surfaced almost overnight in response to a negative story in *American Banker*, the Comptroller's staff had not had an opportunity to find the bank was book insolvent.

The second is *liquidity insolvency*—a bank cannot raise sufficient cash to pay its obligations as they become due. There was not a liquidity insolvency at Penn Square because the Fed had been lending it sufficient money to meet its obligations.

The bank would open on Tuesday, July 6, unless the Comptroller found insolvency. The Federal Reserve threatened to continue lending to the bank. If this happened, the bank's remaining uninsured depositors would flee and be replaced by fully collateralized loans from the Fed. When the bank was finally closed for good, the FDIC, after paying off the insured depositors, would be the only remaining unsecured creditor. Our losses would be increased enormously.

I wrote a letter to Paul Volcker and had it delivered by messenger. I said that if the Federal Reserve allowed Penn Square to reopen after the weekend and continued to fund it, the FDIC would challenge the validity of the Fed's lien against the bank's assets. Paul was not the least bit happy when he called.

"I got your letter," he said in his deep, booming voice. "I don't think you want to challenge our lien. It would set a very bad precedent."

"I agree, Paul," I responded. "I have no interest in challenging the Fed's lien, but it's not an acceptable outcome for the Fed to allow uninsured depositors to run at great cost to the FDIC."

As the debate raged through the weekend, the FDIC's staff was struggling to figure out how to cope with a failure of this magnitude. We had never paid off insured depositors in a bank larger than $100 million. Worse, this failure was sprung on the FDIC overnight, and we had almost no information about the bank.

I walked into a very somber FDIC staff meeting in a large conference room across the hall from my office. The latest was that Penn Square's data processing was handled by an outside firm, and the firm was closed for the holiday weekend. Unless we could get to the bank's records right away, there would be no hope of having checks ready for the depositors by July 6.

This bank failure was certain to receive nationwide media attention. The last thing we wanted was for bank customers throughout the nation to see on television crowds of angry depositors milling around a closed Penn Square Bank unable to get to their money. We had to get the checks ready by July 6.

I asked Jim Davis, the head of the FDIC's liquidation staff, if they had been able to reach anyone from the data processing company. He reported they had talked with a senior person, but the staff was on holiday and scattered.

"Tell the guy he's got to get this job done for us right away," I snapped. "Offer to pay his people double time, offer him a $100,000 bonus, but don't take 'no' for an answer."

I could feel the atmosphere change in the room. The staff was used to doing things by the book. I just told them to throw out the book and get the job done.

I received a call on Sunday morning, July 4, asking me to attend a meeting with Secretary of the Treasury Don Regan. I never asked how the meeting came about, but my guess was that Volcker asked for the session to resolve the dispute between the Fed and the FDIC on how to handle Penn Square.

The Treasury is located in a grand old building right next to the White House, while the FDIC's headquarters is in a 1960s building on the opposite side of the White House. Walking from the FDIC past the White House to the Treasury, you cannot help but feel an enormous sense of history.

Attending the meeting were Volcker, Conover, Fed Vice Chairman Preston Martin, and me. We briefed Regan for about an hour.

Finally, Regan said, "It appears you've considered every angle. Before we make a decision, let me ask if anyone believes the financial system is so fragile that it will not be able to absorb the shock of letting this bank fail?"

Volcker and Martin answered first, saying they believed there was a significant risk that letting Penn Square fail could produce severe shock waves that might not be controllable. Conover said he thought there was no significant risk to the banking system.

I responded last, "I believe there's some risk to the system if we let Penn Square fail. But I believe that risk isn't nearly as great as the risk to the system down the line if we don't let the bank fail. If we bail out a bank that has this much mismanagement and abuse, we'll send a message that anything goes. We'll sanction behavior that could lead to a nationalization of the banking system before we're through."

The room was quiet as we waited for Regan to speak. I assumed he would say something like, "Bill, I agree with your long-run concerns, but let's not make waves right now—let's see if we can arrange a merger for this bank."

I was stunned, elated, and, for the first time, nervous when he said, "Legally, this is the FDIC's call. I have no authority here. Bill, do what you believe is right and let the chips fall where they may."

I raced back to the FDIC and entered the large conference room on the executive floor. The room was packed with senior staff awaiting the results of the meeting. The FDIC had never before stood its ground on how a significant bank failure would be handled. I could tell from the looks on their faces that the staff was sure this time would be no different.

I said simply, "We got our wish. We're going to do a deposit payoff. We've got a lot of work to do and not much time to do it, so let's get moving."

The room came alive and was energized in an instant.

■■■

I went across the hall to my office, which has one of the most glorious views in Washington, overlooking the White House lawn, the Jefferson Memorial, and the Washington Monument. I had read a fair amount about the banking collapse of the 1930s. Throughout the weekend of debates I had no doubt that we had to let Penn Square fail. I knew it would send ripples through the financial system, but I was certain the system could withstand the shock.

Staring out my windows at the Washington Monument on July 4, 1982, I felt very much alone, exposed, and aware of my youth and relative inexperience. I admired and looked up to, both figuratively and literally, the 6-foot, 7-inch Paul Volcker, who had just declared that he believed that what we were about to do at Penn Square could collapse the financial system.

"What if I'm wrong?" I thought. "What if the shock waves *are* too strong and the system collapses? I'll go down in history as the guy who set off the banking collapse of the 1980s."

Just then Jim Sexton walked up behind me. Jim is a very talented and bright guy who then headed the FDIC's bank supervisory department. We had a close relationship, and he sensed what I was thinking.

He said, "The banking system will be better off in the long run."

Without taking my eyes off the Washington Monument, I answered softly, "I just hope we make it through the short run."

The next week was a blur. We worked around the clock in Washington and Oklahoma to get ready to distribute the checks to insured depositors on Tuesday morning. We had gotten the data processor to produce the computer runs we needed.

We chartered two small jets to take some key FDIC staff and me to Oklahoma on the evening of July 5. I raced home to get some clothes, and the planes left around midnight. The night was clear with a full moon and the flight was smooth. Thank goodness for that, because a ruptured disc in my back was killing me. I had difficulty riding in a car without the searing pain bringing tears to my eyes.

We arrived in Oklahoma City around five o'clock in the morning. What I did not need was a chatty cab driver, but as luck would have it, I got one anyway. Driving to the hotel, he asked what I did for a living.

"I'm in banking," I said.

The cabbie shot back, "Banking is a great racket. It's like having a license to steal. There's no way you can lose."

I wonder if he ever discovered who his passenger was and the reason for my visit to Oklahoma City.

We had scheduled an early morning press conference, so there was no point trying to sleep. I showered and got dressed. In my rush to throw together some clothes for the trip, I had forgotten dress socks. I borrowed a pair—the wrong color—from an FDIC colleague. The day was not starting well.

The press conference drew a large crowd of both print and broadcast media. Toward the end of the conference, a reporter noted that Penn Square's troubles surfaced, and the run by depositors had begun after a negative article in the *American Banker*. The reporter asked if I blamed the media for the failure.

I looked at Phil Zweig, who was sitting about five rows back. Zweig was the reporter who broke the Penn Square story in the *American Banker* and later wrote an acclaimed book about it called *Belly Up*. He looked like he was trying to find a way to hide under his chair.

"No. The media had a job to do," I responded, "and they did it well. Penn Square would have failed anyway, and I'd rather have it happen sooner than later."

I looked back at a beaming Zweig.

I went to the shopping center where Penn Square Bank was located. The line of depositors was very long but orderly. We had done it—they were getting their checks!

■■■

The Penn Square failure broke new ground in several respects. It was the first time the FDIC decided how it would handle a significant bank failure without abiding by the wishes of the central bank. That was an important and positive development in my view. The central bank's primary focus is on monetary policy and price stability. It does not like volatility in the markets and will always prefer a major bank failure to be handled in the least disruptive way. That is an important point of view, but should not control every decision.

I believe it is essential to have private sector discipline at work in the financial system. The only way that can happen is if the private sector is at risk in a meaningful way. This means that generally creditors should lose some money when a bank fails, even though it will be disruptive.

Of course, there may come a time when the problems in the system are so pervasive that the system really cannot withstand any more disruption and instability. I did not believe Penn Square was the place to draw that line.

Penn Square had $500 million of deposits at the time of its failure, divided roughly equally between insured and uninsured. The FDIC paid off the insured depositors at the time of failure and stepped into their shoes. We estimated that the uninsured depositors would ultimately receive 80 cents recovery on each dollar they had on deposit above the $100,000 insurance limit.

To alleviate the disruption and pain associated with the Penn Square failure, we implemented a new technique for making funds available more quickly to the uninsured depositors. This method was the precursor of the modified payoff technique we began using the following year. We distributed receivership certificates to the uninsured depositors in the face amount of their uninsured deposits. The FDIC and other bank regulators agreed to value those certificates for bank examination purposes at 80 cents on the dollar. Moreover, the Federal Reserve agreed to make advances through its discount window against those certificates equal to 80 cents on the dollar.

This meant that the uninsured depositors of Penn Square had immediate access to 80 percent of their $250 million in uninsured deposits. We ultimately recovered about 85 cents on the dollar at Penn Square, so uninsured depositors in the end lost just $38 million.

We decided to issue checks to depositors at Penn Square on July 6, come hell or high water. We could not risk television coverage of angry depositors unable to get their money, because depositors at banks around the country might panic.

So we began the deposit payoff without taking the time to balance the bank's books or doing the customary reconciliations and setoffs on the deposit accounts. To make a long story short, we wound up paying about $40 million more to depositors than we should have, and it took us more than a million dollars of accounting fees and six months of effort to get the books to balance. While we recovered most of the money in the end, the situation for the FDIC staff was intense and full of anxiety.

I received a call a few days after the failure from the FDIC person in charge of the Penn Square liquidation. He was trying to tell me about his concerns. He was so incoherent I had trouble following the conversation. A couple of days later he took a medical leave to recover from exhaustion.

A few days after that episode, I experienced severe chest pains on the way home from work. I had the driver take me to Arlington Hospital, where I spent the next several hours undergoing cardiac testing. They could not find anything wrong and concluded the pains were stress induced. We were getting the job done, but at a cost.

■■■

The two most senior officials at the central bank had argued that if the FDIC allowed Penn Square to fail, the banking system might collapse. Following the Penn Square failure, some major banks had difficulty obtaining funding and the cost of their borrowings went up. I was more than a little anxious. The funds markets settled down after a week or so. The system withstood the Penn Square failure.

I shake my head when I hear pundits and politicians talk about how we are going to get rid of "too big to fail." A tiny shopping center bank in Oklahoma City I never heard of until five days before its failure damn near brought down the financial system and would have if we had not handled the aftermath extremely well over the next couple of years after the failure.

The FDIC and the Fed are strong, independent agencies that have a great deal of experience in crisis resolution. One of the worst things Congress could do in the wake of the 2008 crisis is to curtail their authorities to act decisively in a crisis.

At one point during the 1982 Fourth of July weekend debate, Paul Homan from the Comptroller's Office slammed his fist on the table and yelled:

"Dammit, you've got to bail out Penn Square! If you don't, SeaFirst and Continental Illinois will go down!"

The head of the FDIC is treated by staff in much the same manner as a general. I was addressed as "Mr. Chairman" and accorded great deference. None of that for Homan—he was steaming.

"Paul," I said after recovering from the initial shock of his outburst, "if Continental or SeaFirst fails, we'll stop the ripples at that point. But we're not going to protect those banks from feeling the pain of their mistakes at Penn Square."

■■■

In 1983, not long after Penn Square, we were called upon to honor my words of reassurance to Homan. SeaFirst Bank in Seattle purchased a lot of bad loans from Penn Square and had plenty of other bad loans as well. As SeaFirst's problems became public, the bank had trouble borrowing money. The marketplace was imposing its discipline.

SeaFirst replaced its CEO and brought in Dick Cooley, a seasoned and well-respected banker from Wells Fargo Bank. Cooley visited me at the FDIC and said the problems at SeaFirst were worse than he had thought. SeaFirst was experiencing severe liquidity problems, and Cooley wanted to know if the FDIC would provide financial assistance. I responded that we had anticipated the problems at SeaFirst and were prepared to help.

We moved immediately to put in place a $500 million subordinated loan from the FDIC to SeaFirst. The documents were prepared and signed in a matter of days and put in safekeeping. The money would be wired on request, but I cautioned Cooley not to request the money unless the bank needed it desperately.

"Once you draw down the money," I admonished, "you'll have 90 days to find a solution and get the FDIC repaid. If you don't, the bank will be ours, and we'll implement whatever solution we believe appropriate."

The SeaFirst assistance package was never made public and the money was never drawn down. Cooley offered the bank to potential purchasers. I thought he did not have a prayer of getting the bank sold, but Bank of America bought it.

Everything worked out well from the FDIC's standpoint. The shareholders and management of SeaFirst paid for the mistakes made at Penn Square and elsewhere and the problems were resolved without loss to the FDIC. All creditors were made whole, a major failure was averted, and the financial markets remained calm. The assistance package we worked out for SeaFirst would serve as a model for what was to come at Continental Illinois.

As I watched the crisis unfold in 2008, I was dumbstruck by the apparent lack of planning and of a coherent strategy—it seemed like utter chaos. While it is difficult to know precisely which firms will go over the edge and when, there should be a good sense of what might happen and serious contingency planning should take place. Certainly the short sellers had Lehman Brothers and Washington Mutual in their sights long before they crashed—just as the FDIC had SeaFirst and Continental Illinois in its sights as early as July 1982.

■■■

The utter surprise of the Penn Square failure and the lack of information about the bank and its linkages to major banks caused enormous problems for the FDIC. It focused my attention on the

40

fact that the FDIC had no presence at all in the one-third of the nation's banks that held two-thirds of the banking assets.

While the FDIC had authority to examine any insured bank, it traditionally deferred to the Federal Reserve and the Comptroller's Office. The FDIC stayed out of banks supervised by those agencies—national banks and state-chartered Federal Reserve member banks—and contented itself with examining small state banks in which the FDIC's exposure was realistically minimal.

I resolved to change that after Penn Square. We approached the Federal Reserve and the Comptroller's Office about having FDIC personnel join them in their examinations. We wanted to focus on larger banks, troubled banks, and a random sample of other banks. We would blend a few FDIC people into their examination teams, and the Fed and Comptroller would continue to organize and lead the examinations. All we wanted was first-hand knowledge of the institutions.

Nothing is more sacred in Washington than "turf." It would have gone down easier with the leadership at the Fed and the Comptroller's Office if I had said I wanted their first-born children.

The Fed's initial reaction was to brush off the FDIC—surely the FDIC and its chairman were jesting. The Comptroller's Office, still smarting from the blasting it received in congressional hearings on Penn Square, went ballistic—the FDIC would enter a national bank if and only if the Comptroller deemed it appropriate!

It was clear that reason and gentle persuasion were not going to get the job done. I asked the FDIC staff to compile a list of the national and Fed member banks we wanted to learn more about during the coming year. I gave the list to the Fed and the Comptroller and told them the FDIC planned to examine the banks on the list. We preferred to do it as part of the Fed's and Comptroller's teams, but the FDIC would examine the banks.

The media had a field day reporting on the intramural turf war—the story landed on the front page of the *Washington Post*. The Comptroller asked the Department of Justice to sue on behalf of the Comptroller to prevent the FDIC from entering a national bank. The Department of Justice apparently was appalled at the thought of it.

The FDIC prevailed in the end. We routinely joined the Comptroller's Office and the Fed in their examinations of select national and Fed member banks. The program went smoothly and created no confusion or additional burdens.

■■■

Years later, in the wake of the S&L debacle, Congress strengthened the FDIC's hand. It removed whatever doubt might have existed about the FDIC's authority to examine any bank any time and gave the FDIC additional enforcement powers.

It is remarkable just how sacred turf is in Washington and how long-term the memories are. My successor's successor as chairman of the FDIC, Bill Taylor, died far too young at age 52 from complications following surgery, leaving a vacancy in the FDIC chairmanship for nearly two years. Not long after Bill's death, another FDIC director, C. C. Hope, died. The FDIC board, which at this time was supposed to be five members, was down to three. Two of the three worked for the Treasury— namely, the Comptroller and the Director of the Office of Thrift Supervision (OTS).

The Comptroller of the Currency, Eugene Ludwig, seized this opportunity in 1993—a full decade after I secured the right of the FDIC to examine national banks—to give the FDIC a little payback. A majority of the FDIC's three-member board rescinded the FDIC's program of accompanying the Comptroller, the OTS, and the Fed on examinations. The board resolution provided that joint exams could not be conducted without prior approval from the FDIC's board. I called Ludwig and urged him to back off, to no avail.

Because of continuous vacancies on the FDIC board, the FDIC board could not muster the votes to override this restriction until 2004. The banking industry's principal watchdog, the FDIC, was neutered for over a decade during the high growth period in banking leading up to the crisis of 2008.

It presents a fundamental and dangerous conflict for the Comptroller and the OTS, whose banks the FDIC is charged with overseeing, to sit on the FDIC board. The FDIC should have a completely independent board composed of three presidentially appointed members. This reform is far more important than most of the other reforms currently under consideration by Congress.

■■■

It would be difficult to say who was most angry with me following the failure of Penn Square—the citizens of Oklahoma City or the staff of the Comptroller's Office. Someone from the Comptroller's Office must have been very upset indeed, judging by a document leaked to the press shortly after the Penn Square failure.

I received an urgent call one afternoon from Joe Hutnyan, the Washington bureau chief for *American Banker*, asking to see me right away. He sat in a chair in front of my desk and handed me a memo he said he received anonymously.

The memo was an internal FDIC document prepared weekly for the board members. It listed some 50 banks the FDIC believed might fail in the next several months, including the estimated failure dates. I could tell from the markings on the memo that this copy came from the Comptroller's Office. I am sure I must have turned ashen as the blood drained from my face.

"I'm not going to lie," I said to Joe, "this is the real deal. What do you plan to do with it?"

He replied, "I'm not sure. That's what I want to talk to you about. What do you think I should do with it?"

"I have no right to ask you not to publish it," I responded, "but I can tell you that if you do, I have no idea how we'll cope with the fallout. Every bank on the list will fail immediately, and we simply can't handle 50 simultaneous bank failures. It'll be a real mess, and public confidence in the FDIC will likely evaporate. Also, you need to know that a number of these banks will never fail if you don't publish the memo. In the normal course, they'll resolve their problems."

Hutnyan called the editor-in-chief of *American Banker*, and the three of us talked for about an hour. We settled on an approach I felt was fair and appropriate. They would run a story reporting on the leaked memo. The story would reveal the number and size of the banks, but not their names. The story ran the next day and caused no problem—a disaster was narrowly averted.

I could not believe anyone in a banking agency could have been so thoroughly irresponsible. From that point forward, the memo on potential bank failure activity was distributed only to the chairman, and I reported orally to the other board members.

■■■

The citizens of Oklahoma City were able to get their shot at me a few months later. Senators David Boren (D-Okla.) and Don Nickles (R-Okla.) asked if I would attend a town meeting in Oklahoma City to address the concerns of Penn Square's former deposit and loan customers.

I was nervous about doing it because the level of antagonism in Oklahoma toward the FDIC and me was very high. The public chose not to blame the management that created the Penn Square debacle. Instead, it focused its anger on the agency that came in under extraordinarily difficult circumstances to get the depositors their money.

Part of the reason for the anger was that the failure of Penn Square signaled the end of the speculative boom in the oil patch. It had been a very heady ride, and it had come to an abrupt halt. Oil rigs, which had been in short supply for more than a decade, would soon be selling for 10 cents on the dollar. Bumper stickers said, "Please God, Give Us Another Oil Boom—We Promise Not To Piss It Away."

An important reason for the hostility toward the FDIC, quite frankly, was Senator Boren. Oklahoma was entering a very difficult period of economic adjustment. The oil boom was over, and many people and businesses, including many banks, would suffer. The public was looking for someone to blame and politicians were pretty good targets.

Boren decided to give the citizens a different target—the heartless bureaucrats at the FDIC. Boren was a bright, well-educated fellow who later became the president of the University of Oklahoma. He knew the FDIC did not create the mess at Penn Square. He knew the FDIC could not have prevented the speculative bubble in the oil industry from bursting. And he knew the FDIC staff worked night and day to get the depositors of Penn Square their money without delay. Yet Senator Boren took every opportunity to castigate the FDIC in the press.

I decided to do the town meeting primarily because of Senator Nickles. Nickles was aware of the FDIC's unpopularity in Oklahoma, but he did not fan the flames.

I was nervous about the meeting. People who lose everything in an economic collapse can be overwrought with grief and anger. They may want to strike out at someone. A couple of years before Penn Square, a homebuilder who had gone bankrupt in the high interest climate of the late 1970s walked into the Federal Reserve in Washington with a shotgun and with sticks of dynamite strapped to his body. A couple of years after Penn Square, in the middle of the agricultural bank crisis, an FDIC liquidation office in Nebraska was firebombed.

The FDIC staff called the Secret Service to see if we could get some protection for the meeting. They said they had no authority to provide security at the meeting, but they recommended that I be outfitted with a bulletproof vest and that we contact the governor's office in Oklahoma for security.

I walked into the meeting room wearing a bulletproof vest under my shirt accompanied by four of the largest men I have ever seen. The room was jammed with some 1,500 people. I was booed and jeered at every turn, but thankfully there was no physical violence.

Chapter 5

The Butcher Empire Collapses

Immediately before my appointment to the FDIC, I spent four years with the largest bank in Kentucky—First Kentucky. Two prominent and larger-than-life Tennessee bankers, Jake and C. H. Butcher, had borrowed a fair amount of money from First Kentucky and other banks to finance their acquisitions of some 40 banks in Tennessee, Kentucky, and other states.

When interest rates skyrocketed in the late 1970s, I worried about the ability of the Butchers to service their huge debts. On the heels of First Pennsylvania's collapse, I spoke with Irv Sprague about the need to keep a close eye on the Butcher banks. As far as I know, he took no action.

After I became chairman, one of the Butcher banks submitted an application for a merger. It came to the board with a unanimous recommendation for approval from the staff. I objected that I was not comfortable with the application and removed it from the agenda.

Following the meeting, I shared with the staff my concerns about the Butchers' financial position, which I suspected might be precarious in view of the high interest rates and poor economy. I asked them to go over everything carefully before bringing the application back to the board.

They spent the next couple of months reviewing the financial condition of the Butchers and their banks. They exacted a number of commitments from the Butchers to clean up problems and add capital. Finally, the staff said we had no choice but to put the application back on the board agenda and approve it.

We approved the application at the next meeting, but I still was not satisfied that we knew enough about the Butcher banks. We needed to get a picture of the entire enterprise instead of reviewing it one bank at a time, so I asked the staff to commence simultaneous examinations of the major Butcher banks.

About six months later, in late 1982, we had a meeting in Memphis of the heads of the FDIC's regional offices. Dave Meadows, then director of our Memphis region, asked if I would stop by his office. He said we were nearly finished examining the 12 largest Butcher banks. The largest, United American Bank, or UAB, appeared badly insolvent.

About a month later, UAB filed with the FDIC its call report, a financial statement all banks are required to submit periodically. Our examination was finished, so the Butchers knew the FDIC had found UAB insolvent. The call report—a public document—showed the bank with plenty of capital.

Up to this time, bank regulators had always handled troubled banks quietly and out of public view. We asked UAB to amend the report. It refused. UAB brought in its lawyers and accountants to help us see the error of our ways, but we were not convinced.

The FDIC initiated an enforcement action ordering UAB to amend its call report. The bank sought a court injunction. Word of the legal action leaked, and a run by depositors began just before Valentine's Day 1983.

As luck would have it, the FDIC's management committee was meeting at a country inn over a hundred miles from Washington when the run began. Conference calls and speakerphones were not available, so only one of us could participate in each call. We could not leave for Washington because we were in the middle of a blizzard. It was beyond frustrating—maddening might better describe the experience.

We managed to initiate the bidding process to sell UAB. We were going to use for the first time the procedures enacted by Congress in 1982 that permitted us to offer a large failed bank to out-of-state bidders. The snow ended that evening, allowing us to crawl back to Washington for a long weekend sleeping in our offices.

There were three principal bidders for UAB: First Tennessee, the largest bank in the state; C&S Bank, the largest bank in neighboring Georgia; and First Union, one of the largest banks in North Carolina. I preferred to sell to C&S or First Union, all things being equal, because it would further the cause of breaking down barriers to interstate banking that existed at the time.

C&S submitted the most attractive bid and First Union the least attractive, with First Tennessee in between. The Comptroller's Office was not comfortable with C&S's condition and wanted the bank to commit to increase its capital. C&S and the Comptroller's Office argued, while we twiddled our thumbs.

We could not wait any longer, so I set a deadline for them to resolve their dispute. They did not, so we approved First Tennessee's proposal, a deal unlike any we had ever done. We worked around the clock to get the transaction put together over the weekend.

■ ■ ■

We got it done, but doing such a complex deal in such a hurry nearly proved disastrous for First Tennessee. A few months later, I learned from our staff that First Tennessee made a mistake in structuring the transaction. It was likely to wipe out First Tennessee's earnings for the current year and the next two years as well. I called Ron Terry, First Tennessee's CEO.

"I understand you cut a bad deal," I said to Terry after a few pleasantries.

He replied, "Yes, and we're just sick about it. It'll probably wipe out three years' earnings."

"Neither of us intended the deal to work that way," I responded. "Send your people to Washington, and we'll make it right."

My view was that we had to be completely honorable and fair in our dealings with bidders. It was the right thing to do, and it was the only policy that would encourage bidders to deal with us on complex transactions under severe time pressures.

■ ■ ■

I spent a fair amount of time during the weekend of UAB's failure dealing with politicians concerned about the Butchers, who were very prominent in Democratic circles. Jake Butcher had run for governor of Tennessee, and both he and his brother had been major contributors to political candidates.

Tennessee Senator Jim Sasser, a Democrat who went on to be ambassador to China, worried that we were picking on the Butchers because they were prominent Democrats. Even Howard Baker, the Senate's Republican majority leader from Tennessee, and a friend of mine, voiced concerns.

These people knew, liked, and trusted the Butchers. The Butchers had promoted civic causes and business activities in

Tennessee for years. Among other things, they had brought the World's Fair to the state. It was difficult for people to accept that their empire was a house of cards.

A friend from First Kentucky joined UAB as its president a couple of years before it failed. Months after the failure, I called to find out how he and his wife were doing and to explain that he would be a defendant in a suit by the FDIC against the officers and directors of UAB. He told me that when UAB failed, he too thought the closing was politically motivated. He had since come to realize the bank was badly insolvent.

Any lingering doubt he or anyone else might have had about the FDIC's objectivity in blowing the whistle on the Butchers was eliminated a year or so later. Jake and C. H. Butcher pled guilty to criminal charges and served time in prison. One of their business associates committed suicide.

■■■

Following UAB's failure, we spent several months handling the failures, and trying to avoid the failures, of dozens of other Butcher banks in several states. To his credit, C. H. Butcher devoted considerable time in the months following the failure of UAB to helping the FDIC untangle the mess. It might seem odd under the circumstances, but he spent hour upon hour with FDIC staff at our headquarters in Washington.

The Butcher banks were completely intertwined. Indeed, that was how they were able to hide their problems for so long. If a regulator found problems during an examination of a Butcher bank and ordered the problems corrected, the Butchers were always very responsive. The problems were cleaned up, capital was added, and any other steps demanded were taken without hesitation. What we did not and could not know, until we conducted a simultaneous examination of the major Butcher banks, is that the problems being cleaned up were in reality being shifted from one bank to another.

The Butchers had a high profile, so congressional hearings on the collapse of their empire were inevitable. The FDIC was criticized from all directions. About a third of the representatives thought we had been too aggressive in dealing with the Butchers because they were prominent Democrats. Another third thought we had been too lax in dealing with the Butchers because they were prominent Democrats. The remainder seemed genuinely interested in learning how the problems occurred and might have been detected earlier.

My view is that the FDIC could have found the problems earlier had it heeded the warning signs. Once the agency focused on the Butchers, it did a terrific job of uncovering and dealing with the problems. The simultaneous examinations, for example, occupied 10 percent of the FDIC's examination force for over six months. When the examinations were completed, the FDIC demanded that UAB disclose publicly its insolvency, something bank regulators were not accustomed to doing.

■■■

My experience with the Butcher banks is one of the reasons I am such a proponent of consolidating supervision of holding companies and their subsidiaries. Under current U.S. law, bank holding companies are supervised by the Fed while their bank subsidiaries are supervised by whatever agency has jurisdiction over them. For example, Bank of America's holding company is supervised by the Fed while its lead bank is supervised by the Comptroller of the Currency.

I believe this system is terribly flawed and have been urging that a single agency supervise the entire enterprise. This, of course, raises big turf issues, not to mention fear of the unknown, so it is exceedingly difficult to accomplish politically. If the latest debacle in our financial system does not spur Congress to reform the agency structure, I guess nothing will.

Chapter 6

Deposit Insurance Reform / Tackling Wall Street

The State of New York implemented the first deposit insurance plan in the 1820s, and other states followed. While some of the state-sponsored plans worked reasonably well, they lacked the diversification necessary for any insurance system to succeed. The agricultural depression during the otherwise prosperous 1920s wiped out what remained of the state plans.

More than 150 proposals for federal deposit insurance were introduced in Congress between the Civil War and 1930. The stock market crash of 1929, followed by the Great Depression, led to the failure of some 9,000 small banks, about one-third of the banks in the country. Calls for federal deposit insurance, led by Senator Carter Glass (D-Va.), reached a crescendo in 1933.

President Roosevelt and the American Bankers Association were opposed. They believed the plan would be unduly expensive and would require strong, well-managed banks to subsidize weak, poorly managed banks. They wanted the banking industry to restructure itself through nationwide branch banking, which would allow stronger banks to acquire weaker ones.

The proponents of deposit insurance won the day. A compromise was worked out involving a limited depositor protection plan of $2,500 per account. It was accompanied by an array of restrictions to limit the moral hazard from deposit insurance. Deposit interest rate ceilings were imposed, entry into banking was tightly controlled, branching by banks remained very limited, and the permissible activities of banks were curtailed, including requiring the separation of commercial banking from investment banking.

The deposit insurance scheme worked reasonably well for nearly a half century. Bankers were so scarred by the Great Depression they would not have taken on much risk even if there had been no restrictions on their activities.

■ ■ ■

By the time I became chairman of the FDIC, the climate had changed dramatically. The deposit insurance limit had jumped to $100,000 per depositor. Worse yet, the FDIC had adopted the practice of arranging mergers for failing banks. All depositors and other creditors were protected, no matter how large their claim against the bank. Before the Penn Square failure, the FDIC had never enforced the deposit insurance limit in a bank larger than $100 million in deposits.

At the same time the scope of deposit insurance was expanding, competitive pressures pushed banks to accept more risk. Many of the banks' best customers turned elsewhere for their financial needs and profit margins narrowed. Banks solicited new, higher-risk loan customers, reduced their capital cushion, became more aggressive with their investment portfolios, and shortened the maturity of their borrowed funds.

President Roosevelt's nightmare had become a reality. Weak banks and thrifts were being subsidized by strong institutions. The marketplace was imposing little discipline and the risks in the system were growing exponentially. We at the FDIC were very troubled by these developments.

Congress passed the Garn–St. Germain Act in 1982, giving S&Ls broader powers. It would have been an excellent move a decade earlier, but not in 1982, when most S&Ls were essentially broke. We persuaded Congress to add to the Garn–St. Germain Act a provision requiring the deposit insurance agencies to submit reports to Congress on how the deposit insurance system should be reformed in a deregulated banking environment.

The FDIC submitted its report in early 1983. We acknowledged that federal deposit insurance served the nation well during the first 50 years of its existence. The events of the previous few years and the evolving process of deregulation had caused the FDIC to reexamine the role of deposit insurance. We urged Congress to consider reforms to place uninsured depositors and other creditors at greater risk and requested authority to vary insurance premiums with the riskiness of the bank.

Finally, we decided we could not wait for Congress to act on deposit insurance reforms. Deregulation of deposit interest rates required that we find ways to increase the discipline imposed on banks by large depositors and other creditors. To allow banks and S&Ls to pay whatever they chose to attract deposits and then protect all depositors against the risk of loss was a prescription for disaster.

■ ■ ■

Following the Penn Square failure, we developed in 1983 a technique we called the *modified payoff*. A *payoff*, in FDIC parlance, means the FDIC pays off insured depositors and exposes uninsured depositors to the risk of loss. The uninsured creditors await their recovery from the proceeds of the liquidation of the bank's assets. We modified that procedure in Penn Square by estimating what the uninsured creditors would ultimately receive from the liquidation and paying them that amount up front.

The modified payoff gave us the ability to impose the risk of loss on larger creditors without creating a serious liquidity problem in the community. We decided to use it in larger and larger bank failures. Uninsured depositors and other creditors would ultimately get the message that they needed to be careful about the quality of their banks. From 1982 to 1984 we used the modified payoff technique more than a dozen times. We were finding ways to increase market discipline without congressional action.

■ ■ ■

I did not realize it at the time, but I was about to embark on what would become the most politically charged issue of my chairmanship—brokered deposits. Ironically, the issue arose at least in part from the manner in which we handled Penn Square.

Following Penn Square, we began to notice that failed banks nearly always had brokered funds on deposit. Money brokers, ranging from the major Wall Street firms to fly-by-night companies operating from someone's home, were soliciting tens of billions of dollars from the public. They promised to deposit the money in fully insured accounts at banks and S&Ls that paid the highest interest rates. Who could resist the lure of the highest rates in the land with no risk?

Generally, banks and thrifts that paid the highest rates and attracted most of the brokered funds were the weakest, highest-risk institutions. The more discipline we attempted to impose on larger depositors, the more they turned to money brokers to protect them from risk.

Money brokers were able to obtain full insurance for their deposits because the FDIC had interpreted its law to allow pass-through insurance coverage. The money broker was not deemed by the FDIC to be the depositor. Instead, deposit insurance coverage passed through to the investors who gave money brokers the funds.

So, if I had $500,000 I wanted to invest at the highest interest rate available without any risk, I would give it to a money broker. The broker would collect millions or even billions of dollars from people like me and then offer the funds to banks that paid the highest rates. A single broker could deposit tens of millions in a single bank and get full insurance coverage.

We had to find a way to stop this massive abuse. Deposit insurance was intended to protect small depositors placing funds in community banks, not high-rolling investors willing to ship their money anywhere in search of high yields.

■■■

The most effective solution appeared to be to correct the problem at its source. We decided to propose a regulation eliminating pass-through insurance coverage. The money broker would be deemed the depositor and would be limited to $100,000 protection per bank instead of hundreds of millions.

We could not act alone, though. We needed the FSLIC, which insured the S&L industry, to join us in the proposed regulation. If the FSLIC did not join, money brokers would simply place their deposits in S&Ls instead of banks. Taxpayers would still be exposed to the risk of loss through FSLIC insurance, and FDIC-insured banks would be angry because S&Ls would have an advantage in competing for brokered funds.

Ed Gray was chairman of the Federal Home Loan Bank Board, which oversaw the FSLIC. He was from California and had been involved politically with Ronald Reagan for years.

Gray, a very pleasant and conscientious individual, had no experience in the banking or the S&L business before his appointment to head the Bank Board a year or so earlier. Before that, he had been a marketing executive and had served on the White House staff.

He inherited an incredible mess when he stepped into the Bank Board post. I invited him to the FDIC for lunch shortly after his appointment. I told him the S&Ls were in horrible shape and getting worse by the day and urged him to be aggressive in dealing with the S&L problems even though it would be unpopular politically. I learned from Ed later that he had been annoyed by the pep talk and thought I had been condescending.

I had not spoken to Gray much since that lunch and did not know how he would react to my suggestions for dealing with the money brokers. I feared he would not be willing to take on such a politically powerful constituency, particularly since many of the S&Ls were using brokered funds to fuel their growth.

Gray's initial reaction was cautious, but he was willing to explore the subject. After several meetings and briefings, he was convinced that we had to deal with the problem and that elimination of pass-through insurance was the best solution.

The FDIC and FSLIC issued for public comment a proposed regulation to eliminate pass-through deposit insurance coverage, and all hell broke loose. Several major Wall Street firms asked for a meeting with the FDIC to express their displeasure.

To say the meeting did not go well would be a gross understatement. Early on, the CEO of one major investment bank asked how we could have issued the proposed regulation without first consulting with his firm. While I have witnessed a lot during my years in Washington, that statement gets the grand prize for bald arrogance.

The FDIC and FSLIC had given a great deal of thought before issuing our proposed regulation for comment. We received no information in the comment period we had not already considered, so we adopted the final regulation without much change.

Congress called a hearing to criticize the FDIC and FSLIC for picking on the Wall Street firms. I was asked how we could justify interfering with the practice of money brokers making it possible for all Americans to enjoy the highest interest rates available without incurring risk. I retorted that we had no objection to money brokers placing funds in banks and S&Ls. We simply wanted the brokers, who were handling billions of dollars and were very sophisticated, to have an incentive to deal only with the soundest banks and S&Ls, not the weakest.

I believed strongly—and still do—that the practice of money brokers placing billions risk-free in banks and S&Ls represented a massive abuse of the deposit insurance system. I attached to my testimony a schedule detailing dozens of failed banks in which money brokers had placed substantial deposits. I cited by name S&Ls that were borrowing billions from brokers to invest in junk bonds, placing taxpayers at risk. All of this fell on deaf congressional ears.

The Reagan Administration, too, was very unhappy with Ed Gray and me. The Treasury openly criticized our regulation— something I considered highly inappropriate. It occurred to me that Treasury Secretary Don Regan had been the CEO of the largest money broker—Merrill Lynch—before entering government service, but I was assured that Don had recused himself from involvement in the money broker issue.

The Wall Street firms were relentless. They took out ads in the *Wall Street Journal* and the *New York Times* condemning the FDIC's "Sledge Hammer Rule"—"Why Use a Sledge Hammer to Kill a Fly When a Fly Swatter Will Do?"

Several firms filed suit against the FDIC and FSLIC, contending we lacked authority to adopt the new regulation. I had no doubt the regulation would be upheld based on discussions with our lawyers.

I was bitterly disappointed when the U.S. Circuit Court of Appeals for the District of Columbia agreed with the money brokers and struck down our regulation. We asked Congress to amend the law to allow us to eliminate pass-through insurance, but we might as well have asked for the moon.

We continued to do whatever we could to slow down the rush of brokered funds into banks. We took enforcement actions against problem banks to prohibit them from accepting any further brokered funds—a lot like closing the barn door after the horses are gone, but better than nothing.

We issued a press release every time a bank failed, listing by name the money brokers that had deposited funds in the bank. We also slowed down the payments to money brokers when a bank failed until after we had done a thorough investigation to determine whether there was any fraud in connection with the brokered funds.

We did whatever we could, but we were clearly swimming against the tide. Almost immediately after I left the FDIC at the end of 1985, my successor, Bill Seidman, called a unilateral cease-fire in the battle against the money brokers. A short time later, Ed Gray left the Bank Board and was replaced by Dan Wall, who had no stomach for the fight.

The Wall Street firms had won the war on all fronts. Free to do whatever they wished, they poured tens of billions of dollars into banks and thrifts each month. I do not know how much the money brokers cost taxpayers because the FDIC and FSLIC stopped tracking the flow of funds after Ed Gray and I left. I have no doubt the cost to taxpayers was in the tens of billions of dollars.

Even after Congress finally dealt with the S&L crisis in 1989—by which time taxpayers had lost nearly $150 billion on the S&Ls—it could not muster the courage to face down the money brokers. Rather than eliminating pass-through insurance, Congress simply directed the FDIC to limit the use of brokered funds by problem banks.

I had no idea when I took on the money brokers just how large the stakes were for them. I understood they were earning fees from investors wishing to put their money to work. They were also collecting fees from the banks and thrifts in which they placed the funds. I knew these fees easily exceeded $100 million a year—a large sum of money, but not enough to warrant the all-out war the brokers had declared.

■■■

It was not until later that I realized that I had stepped into the middle of the biggest scam against taxpayers in history—at least up to that point. The Wall Street firms were raising vast amounts of money and selling those funds to banks and thrifts facing severe problems, charging fees on both sides of the deal. Then they were borrowing the funds back from those institutions to finance leveraged buyouts of major companies. If the deals did not work out, the bank or S&L did not collect its loans and we taxpayers were left holding the bag.

The amount of money generated by the Wall Street firms from this scam was almost beyond comprehension. Michael Milken, the "junk bond king" from Drexel Burnham, was paid a salary and bonus of $500 million in just one year! He eventually went to jail for securities fraud, and his firm went bankrupt. Even after paying very substantial fines, he apparently remains a very rich man.

My inability to put a stop to this massive abuse of taxpayers and the deposit insurance system was a bitter disappointment. Looking back, and considering the enormous financial stakes, I understand why we were unable to stop the money brokers. We came close. If not for an incredibly bad decision by the U.S. Court of Appeals and a Congress catering to Wall Street, we and the American taxpayers would have won.

Brokered deposits continue to play an important role in the current banking crisis. They are not prohibited unless and until a bank becomes a problem bank, which leads to a highly procyclical result. Banks load up on brokered deposits during good times, using the money to fund ever-increasing lending activities. When things go south and the bank becomes a problem, the FDIC orders the bank to reduce its brokered deposits and lowers the interest rate that can be paid for them. This creates a severe liquidity crunch for the bank, which frequently leads to its demise.

It would be much sounder for Congress to eliminate pass-through deposit insurance coverage. It should not come as a surprise that this sensible reform is not contained in any of the legislative reform proposals currently under serious consideration by Congress.

■ ■ ■

I took my oath of office to serve a six-year term at the FDIC in March 1978, so my term was set to expire in March 1984. I loved the people at the FDIC and found it extremely challenging and satisfying to lead the agency during the worst banking crisis since the Great Depression. But I did not want to serve another term. I was tired, my personal life needed attention, and it was time to return to the private sector.

While I did not want to serve another six-year term, I did want to be reappointed to the agency by President Reagan. I am a Republican and wanted to be reappointed by a Republican, having been appointed in the first instance by a Democrat. If reappointed, I intended to serve only a year or two of my new term.

I cannot prove that it was the money brokers who kept that from happening, but I am more than a little suspicious that they did. I had gotten along well with the Reagan Administration prior to the battle with the money brokers. I believe strongly in free markets, which put me in sync philosophically with the Reaganites. The Treasury nonetheless made it clear in early 1984 it would not support my reappointment.

Unfortunately for Treasury and the money brokers, I had a trick or two up my own sleeve. A couple of years earlier, Congress had, at my request, changed the FDIC law to provide that board members could remain in office until their successors were appointed and confirmed by the Senate.

Senator Howard Baker (R–Tenn.) was the Senate majority leader and Senator Jake Garn (R–Utah) was the chairman of the Senate Banking Committee. They both believed I was doing a good job at the FDIC.

Baker and Garn wrote the Administration a letter saying the president should not bother sending a nomination to the Senate for a new FDIC chairman. They said they would not schedule a Senate vote on the nominee unless and until I was ready to leave.

We were at a standoff. Treasury was in a position to block my reappointment. I was in a position to remain in the job for as long as I wished. That is where things stood on the eve of the largest bank failure in history up to that time.

Chapter 7

Continental Illinois Topples

When Penn Square failed in 1982 we recognized that at some point we might have to deal with the failure of Continental Illinois, headquartered in Chicago and the country's seventh-largest bank. That point came in May 1984.

While the bailout of First Pennsylvania Bank in 1980 was the first major example of a "too big to fail" bank (and the best example of it, as it was bailed out in every sense of the term), our handling of Continental Illinois imprinted the "too big to fail" doctrine on the public psyche. The doctrine continues to haunt us in the current crisis.

■■■

Continental suffered liquidity pressures in 1982 in the wake of the Penn Square failure, but things settled down. I believed then and continue to believe that Continental could have avoided failure if it had taken decisive steps beginning in 1982.

The prevailing view at the Federal Reserve, and to a lesser extent the Comptroller's Office, was that creditors of banks would not accept a radical overhaul of a major troubled bank. The Fed believed it was important to convey a sense of calm and order at banks, particularly large ones that were heavily dependent on money market sources of funding.

I believed the marketplace could not be lulled to sleep indefinitely, and it would eventually become clear that Continental had serious problems. The markets would be reassured only if they believed the bank's management, board, and regulators were doing everything in their power to correct the problems.

Continental's Penn Square losses were the tip of the iceberg. The bank pursued an aggressive lending strategy for years, and many mistakes were made.

A harmful law in Illinois prohibiting branch banking compounded the troubles. Most banks attract deposits through branches to fund their growth. Without the ability to open branches, Continental had to purchase its funding in the money markets. This type of funding tends to be short-term, expensive, and highly volatile. Continental's funding became even shorter and more expensive after the Penn Square failure exposed the bank's weaknesses.

I argued with the Fed and Comptroller's Office that Continental needed to replace its top management and eliminate its dividend following the Penn Square debacle. If the bank's board would not make these moves, regulators should insist.

Instead, Continental retained its management and maintained its dividend, despite growing loan problems and abysmal earnings. The bank began selling off its readily marketable assets to enhance its capital ratio and support its dividend payments.

Selling off the best assets of a troubled bank can be counter-productive, as what remains is relatively more troubled and has less earning power. The marketplace grew restless—an ominous development for a bank that was so illiquid it had to purchase $8 billion of its funding daily (equal to an astonishing 20 percent of its assets).

Continental announced in early 1984 a last-minute sale of its highly profitable credit card portfolio, which allowed the bank to report a quarterly profit. This proved to be the last straw for the financial markets, as they became convinced Continental was not going to address its problems in a serious fashion.

Rumors about Continental started circulating in financial markets throughout the world, no doubt fueled by investment bankers attempting to interest a foreign bank in buying Continental. Interestingly, a foreign bank could have purchased Continental, but a domestic bank from outside Illinois could not have done so, thanks to a law preventing interstate banking. I am convinced Continental could have been sold to a domestic bank in 1982 or 1983, without FDIC assistance, if the law had permitted it.

■■■

I received a call in May 1984 from Fed chairman Paul Volcker. He asked that I come to his office right away, as a crisis was developing at Continental. Comptroller of the Currency Todd Conover was already there when I arrived.

Continental was experiencing a severe run. Not the old-fashioned kind, in which depositors line up at the teller windows demanding their money. This run was silent and high-tech. Continental went into the markets throughout the world each day to acquire funding. A growing number of suppliers of funds were spooked and were refusing to lend money to Continental. Those that would lend raised their rates.

Volcker said Continental was borrowing some $4 billion from the Fed. The total could easily climb to $10 billion during the next two weeks, and in view of the short-term nature of the bank's liabilities, it could climb to $20 billion during the next month. To put these numbers in perspective, Continental's assets totaled $40 billion, which is equivalent to some $250 billion today. So borrowing $20 billion from the Fed in 1984 is equivalent to borrowing $125 billion or so today.

I had no doubt about what we needed to do. I decided when we handled the Penn Square failure that we would stop the ripple effects from going beyond SeaFirst and Continental.

While I had been confident the system could withstand the failure of Penn Square, I was even more confident the system could not withstand the failure of Continental. Virtually every money center bank in the country was loaded up with loans to less-developed countries and had a lot of other problems. Bank of America, First Chicago, Manufacturers Hanover, Chemical Bank, and Chase Manhattan were among the banks we were worried about.

All of the major banks in Texas and Oklahoma were beginning to show signs of trouble. The S&L industry was in big trouble—so much so that the FSLIC simply did not have the human and financial resources to cope with the situation.

Moreover, some 2,500 small correspondent banks had billions on deposit at Continental. If we allowed Continental to go down, a number of those banks would fail, causing further hardship throughout the already suffering agricultural belt. Indeed, over the next several years, hundreds of agricultural banks failed even though they had been spared losses at Continental.

Volcker, Conover, and I quickly reached agreement on what we needed to do. We had been through a dress rehearsal of sorts with SeaFirst Bank. Although it never became necessary to fund the loan, the FDIC agreed to make a $500 million subordinated loan in order to stop a run at SeaFirst. I told Volcker the FDIC would enter into a similar arrangement with Continental so we could buy time for a more permanent solution to the bank's problems.

On Volcker's recommendation, we briefed Treasury Secretary Don Regan before proceeding. Regan was fully supportive, but suggested that the FDIC not act alone on the subordinated loan to Continental. He felt the financial markets would find it reassuring if we recruited a number of major banks to participate in the loan. He also thought the rescue effort would attract less political heat if the private sector joined us. As an important aside, I wish Treasury Secretary Henry Paulson had exhibited a fraction of this wisdom in 2008.

We considered how big the loan would need to be to reassure the public. Our first thought was a $1 billion loan, which we bumped to $2 billion. It did not matter precisely how much it was, as long as it would be viewed by the markets as a very large commitment. We agreed we should err on the high side, because we would be in big trouble if this deal failed to stabilize Continental.

Most of the major U.S. banks were already involved in a private sector $4.5 billion safety net arranged by Morgan Guaranty to help Continental. We asked Morgan's chief executive, Lew Preston, to convene a meeting of seven of the safety net banks to discuss increasing the safety net loan to $5.3 billion and participating in the FDIC loan.

Secrecy was critically important. The last thing we needed was to have some newspaper report that the government was meeting with the chief executives of the major banks to decide whether and how to rescue Continental. This was one scoop Laura Gross and the *American Banker* were not going to get.

We met not at Morgan Guaranty's headquarters, but at a New York City branch office of the bank. Volcker, standing some 6 feet and 7 inches tall, was one of the most recognizable figures in the country, particularly in the nation's financial capital. The trick was to get him into and out of the bank without attracting attention. Having a car take him into the bank's loading dock area used for armored trucks solved the problem.

Volcker briefed the bankers on Continental and told them the FDIC had decided to intervene with temporary assistance to provide the time needed to craft a longer-term solution. When he finished, I was struck by the fact that he did not ask the bankers for anything.

The bankers did not have to be puzzled for very long, as I spoke next and got right to the point. I told them the FDIC would make a $2 billion subordinated loan to Continental, payable on demand, and we wanted the banks to participate to the tune of $500 million. I added that we needed to announce the assistance package before the markets opened the next day, so we had to know their intentions right away.

The responses were immediate and ran the gamut. John McGillicuddy, the head of Manufacturers Hanover, praised the FDIC for being willing to step in and said the industry must do its part to help. Tom Theobald, a top official of Citicorp attending on behalf of CEO Walter Wriston, argued that Continental should be allowed to fail (another of life's ironies, considering the status of Citigroup in the crisis of 2008 and its aftermath). The rest of the bankers fell between those two ends of the spectrum, with everyone willing to consider participating in the rescue effort.

We debated whether the rescue effort could stem the massive outflow of funds from Continental. Continental's borrowings from the Federal Reserve had already climbed above $10 billion, with no end in sight.

I suggested that the FDIC issue a statement that no creditor of Continental would suffer a loss at Continental. The bankers were enthusiastic about the idea, but Volcker was negative. He felt it would set a bad precedent. I countered that we had already made the decision not to let Continental fail, so we ought to make that clear.

I prevailed but still faced hours of wrangling about precisely what the statement would say. Volcker wanted the statement to be vague, and I wanted it to be clear as a bell. We settled on an ambiguously clear statement. The press release announcing the assistance package would contain the following paragraph:

> In view of all the circumstances surrounding Continental Illinois Bank, the FDIC provides assurance that, in any arrangements that may be necessary to achieve a permanent solution, all depositors and other general creditors of the bank will be fully protected and service to the bank's customers will not be interrupted.

That one-sentence paragraph would become the most controversial aspect of the rescue effort. I was raked over the coals at congressional hearings. How could the FDIC protect all depositors of Continental when the statutory deposit insurance limit was $100,000? Where did the FDIC get the authority to protect nondeposit creditors as well?

The answer was pretty simple. We made a decision that the final solution for Continental would not involve a liquidation of the bank and payoff of insured deposits. We might merge Continental with another bank, we might sell it to an investor group with FDIC assistance, or the FDIC might recapitalize the bank. Each of those transactions would automatically protect all general creditors of Continental. So we were not expanding the deposit insurance limit, we were making a commitment regarding the nature of the final solution for Continental.

■■■

We worked through the day to get the terms of the rescue package nailed down. Finally, it appeared to be in good shape with nothing left but the drafting of legal documents. I went to my hotel around midnight.

The ringing phone jarred me about two hours after my head hit the pillow. It was Doug Jones, the FDIC's lead lawyer. Doug, an incredibly good and hard-working lawyer, had FDIC blood in his veins. His father had been an FDIC examiner and Doug's wife was an FDIC lawyer. Doug reported that the deal was coming unglued because of Citicorp.

I returned to the bank and spent the next few hours reviewing the situation. Citicorp was playing hardball and its demands were unacceptable to the FDIC. I waited until about six o'clock to call Volcker. Paul and I called Walter Wriston, Citicorp's chief, at home to complain about Citicorp's behavior. He promised to get it straightened out.

It appeared things were back on track, so I left the bank to catch the shuttle to Washington. We would release the announcement just before the stock market opened.

Before arriving at the airport in New York, I got another call from Doug Jones. Citicorp was back at it. Doug was frustrated, and I was at the end of my rope. We could not wait another day to announce the rescue package, and we had to announce before the markets opened. We wanted all of the major banks on board as a show of solidarity.

We had to get off the dime with Citicorp. I told Doug we would revise the press release to omit the names of the participating banks, so if Citicorp left the consortium it would not be as noticeable.

I added, "Doug, you may quote me on this to Citicorp. Tell them we won't accept their terms, we're going forward with or without them and they can % # @ & * #."

I called Doug when I landed in D.C. to see where things stood. Citicorp had backed down and the deal was set to proceed with Citicorp on board. Did the persuasiveness of our arguments or the expletives win them over, I wondered.

About a year later, John Reed, who succeeded Walter Wriston as the head of Citicorp, visited me. I asked why Citicorp had played hardball on the Continental deal. To my surprise, he said Citicorp believed the government was going to stick the banks with a large loss on Continental, and Citicorp was just trying to protect itself as best it could. I thought we had made it amply clear that we had no intention of sticking it to the rescue banks.

■■■

As Continental Illinois was the seventh-largest bank in the United States, the announcement of the rescue package on May 17, 1984, was big news throughout the world. The "sleepy little agency" it was my privilege to lead was playing in the major leagues, and the stakes were very high.

The next couple of weeks were nerve wracking. Would the markets take enough comfort from the rescue package to put an end to the flight of money from Continental? I received continuous reports on Continental's borrowings from the Fed. They were over $10 billion when the announcement was made and climbed to over $14 billion. Finally, they stabilized. Our temporary package was working!

Shortly after the announcement of the rescue package, I received a call from Volcker. The Federal Reserve Bank of Chicago wanted the FDIC to guarantee its loans to Continental. If we did not, it would file a lien against Continental's assets. I was aghast.

"My God, Paul, we just issued a press release proclaiming to the world that all general creditors of Continental will be protected," I blurted. "We can't expect the private sector to trust us if the Chicago Fed doesn't."

We went around and around. Paul was trying to be helpful, but the Chicago Fed was not willing to keep lending without filing a lien or receiving an FDIC guarantee. I could not let them file a lien in view of the negative message that would convey to the world. We finally resolved it by me sending a private letter to the Chicago Fed guaranteeing that should Continental fail, the FDIC would take over the Fed's loans to the bank.

■■■

The next two months were the busiest, most intense, and challenging period of my life. We worked seven days a week exploring options for achieving a long-term solution to Continental's problems. That was on top of a steady stream of bank failures and the FDIC's normal activities, including congressional hearings.

Several major banks and investor groups approached us about buying Continental. They each wanted a deal in which the FDIC took all of the downside risk and they got the upside. I could not blame them for trying, but they were not going to get that deal. If the FDIC had to take the downside risk, it would get the upside potential.

It became pretty clear by the middle of June that a sale of Continental would not be in the FDIC's economic interest. I directed the staff to continue exploring sale options, but to focus most of their time and energy on developing an FDIC package to put Continental back on its feet.

The package to rehabilitate Continental began to take shape. The FDIC would invest $1 billion in nonvoting, preferred stock of Continental (the law prohibited the FDIC from taking voting stock). The preferred stock would have the right to convert into 160 million shares of common stock, or 80 percent of Continental's outstanding shares. The FDIC would have a great deal of authority over Continental's operations.

The FDIC would acquire $5.1 billion of problem loans from Continental (which had already been written down to $4.5 billion) for a price of $3.5 billion (which meant Continental would have to take another $1.0 billion writedown on the loans). Continental would be paid a fee to manage the collection process on the problem loans, subject to FDIC oversight.

The existing shareholders of Continental would keep up to 20 percent ownership in the company, depending on the FDIC's losses on the problem loans. If the FDIC's losses were zero, the shareholders would keep the entire 20 percent interest. If the FDIC's losses were $800 million or more, the shareholders would forfeit their entire interest to the FDIC. If the FDIC's losses were between zero and $800 million, the shareholders would forfeit a proportionate share of their interest to the FDIC.

The deal was structured this way so the FDIC could treat the shareholders as closely as possible to the way they would have been treated if Continental had failed. At the time of the deal, Continental had capital of $800 million (after the $1 billion loan writeoff and before the FDIC's capital infusion). We would allow Continental's shareholders to maintain an ownership stake to the extent the $800 million was not depleted.

We devised a way to conserve the FDIC's cash, which was a very high priority in view of the enormous problems we were facing throughout the banking system. We needed to invest $1.0 billion in the stock of Continental and pay $3.5 billion for the bad loans. Instead of writing Continental a $4.5 billion check, the FDIC would assume responsibility for repaying $4.5 billion of Continental's borrowings from the Fed. We would pay off the borrowings over time, primarily from collections on the bad loans.

■■■

While the basic structure of the deal was coming together nicely, the deal was not destined to be put to bed so easily. Deputy Secretary of the Treasury Tim McNamar was about to become a pain in our backside.

McNamar was opposed on philosophical grounds to the FDIC putting capital into Continental's parent holding company (where it would be downstreamed as equity to the bank). This would have the effect of bailing out the creditors of the holding company, something McNamar found objectionable. He argued that we should put capital directly into the bank and let the parent company fail.

While I had sympathy for McNamar's philosophical position, his plan was not feasible. The parent company had debt agreements that prohibited what he wanted us to do. The only way we could put money directly into the bank would be as a loan. The bank needed more equity, not debt, to be viable in the financial markets.

Besides, the whole debate was largely academic. The preferred stockholders and creditors of the parent company were minuscule in the scheme of things, and they were likely to receive 100 cents on the dollar in a liquidation of the parent company no matter what we did.

There was no way to convince McNamar. I arrived home from work around midnight on a Saturday to be greeted by a ringing phone. It was McNamar, who was on his way home from some event. We went around and around.

Finally, I cut it off, "Tim, we can talk all night, and I'll never convince you and you'll never convince me. I'm very tired and I'm going to bed. Goodnight."

McNamar was not getting anywhere by either persuasion or intimidation, so he tried a legal challenge. The Treasury asked the Justice Department to issue a legal opinion on whether the FDIC had the authority to infuse capital into a holding company.

I was incensed. I told McNamar that neither Treasury nor the Justice Department had the authority to interpret the FDIC's law. The courts would defer to the FDIC as long as its interpretation of the law was not blatantly wrong.

I added, "I don't really care what opinion Justice issues, we'll do what we believe is best."

I called Volcker to see whether I could back up that statement. We needed the Fed on board to be able to put the deal together.

I said, "Paul, if the Justice Department issues an opinion that the FDIC doesn't have authority to do the transaction as proposed, I plan to go ahead anyway. Can I count on the Fed?"

He hesitated and then replied, "It would be best to get Treasury to support the deal. Let's keep working on that, but if we can't bring them around, we'll support you."

I will always treasure the opportunity I had to work with Paul Volcker. Public servants do not come any better.

Next I called McNamar's boss, Don Regan. I asked if he was aware of the disagreement I was having with McNamar, and he said he was. I told him that try as I might, I could not find a sensible way to do the deal that would satisfy McNamar. Then I put it on the line.

I said, "Don, you've been appointed by the president to oversee the financial system. If you want the deal done Tim's way, I'll defer to you and resign. I'll go quietly and won't criticize anyone. Then you can put someone in here to do whatever deal you want. But I can't stay here and do the deal Tim's way."

He didn't hesitate, "Bill, you're doing a good job, and I don't want you to resign. Do the deal the way you think best, and I'll handle Tim."

With Volcker and Regan pledging their support, it did not really matter what opinion the Justice Department issued. I was pleasantly surprised when the opinion came. It backed the FDIC.

■■■

Before we could announce the Continental restructuring, we had to find a new CEO for the company. We needed someone with a great deal of credibility in banking circles. Volcker, Conover, and I put our heads together and came up with three names: Tom Theobald from Citicorp, Dick Cooley from SeaFirst, and Bill Ogden from Chase.

Having Theobald on the list was the irony of ironies, considering that he had represented Citicorp at our earlier Continental negotiations and had been a real pain in the neck. Having Cooley on the list was also a bit ironic in that we had dealt with him previously on the SeaFirst rescue effort.

We decided that even if we could get one of these bankers to run Continental, we needed to do something to restore Continental's image in the business community in the Midwest. We wanted a business leader from the Chicago area to serve as nonexecutive chairman of the board of Continental. Sy Keene, president of the Federal Reserve Bank of Chicago, suggested John Swearingen.

Swearingen was a legend in Chicago and the oil industry. He was named CEO of Standard Oil of Indiana (renamed Amoco) in his thirties and built it into a powerful and highly successful company. He had just retired and might be available.

I reached Swearingen at his home in Palm Springs. We did not know each other, but our conversation was positive. He agreed to come to Washington to talk further.

I called Theobald to find out if he was interested in the CEO position. He said he had some personal problems and could not consider the job at that time. To add further irony, fast-forward a few years. Theobald is named CEO of Continental to replace the management the FDIC put into place in 1984. He changes the bank's strategy, buys out the FDIC's remaining ownership position in Continental, and sells the company to Bank of America, making a fair amount of money for himself in the process. Not bad for a guy who argued strenuously we should let Continental fail.

I spoke next to Cooley about the CEO position. He was receptive and agreed to come to Washington to negotiate a package. With Swearingen and Cooley both interested and on their way to Washington, this thing was coming together. It seemed too good to be true, and it was.

I met with Cooley and worked out terms—or so I thought. Swearingen decided he needed a greater role than the figurehead chairman of the board role we had in mind. Cooley started to get uncomfortable and turned the contract negotiations over to his lawyer. After several wasted days of trying unsuccessfully to get Cooley back on track, he and I spoke by phone. He said he could not get comfortable and wanted to withdraw.

So we were down to Bill Ogden. Not that he was our third choice. We would have been pleased to have any one of the three.

I approached the other two first only because we thought they were more likely to accept the position than Ogden. We guessed wrong, and it cost us precious time. Both Continental and the FDIC were under a microscope. We needed to get the situation resolved.

I knew Ogden better than I knew Cooley and Theobald. He cared deeply about the banking industry and his country. I told him we needed him to take the position at Continental for the good of the country. If we did not get the bank stabilized, the banking system could topple.

Ogden's only reservation—and it was a big one—was Swearingen. They had served together on the board of Chase Manhattan, and they did not much care for each other.

Swearingen was feeling his oats. He upped the ante and demanded that he be named chairman and CEO. There was no way Ogden would accept Swearingen as his boss.

I was directing a three-ring circus. Swearingen was in one office, Ogden was in another, and the lawyers and investment bankers were in a conference room. I kept going from one office to the next trying to bring closure.

We finally worked out a strange arrangement between Ogden and Swearingen. Ogden would be the CEO of the bank, while Swearingen would be the CEO of the parent company. Neither would be considered the boss of the other.

It was time to make courtesy calls to let congressional leaders and Treasury Secretary Regan know we were about to announce a deal. I explained the plan to Fernand J. St. Germain (D-R.I.), the chairman of the House Banking Committee. Freddie, as he was known, pronounced himself happy and said we had done a great job.

Then he added, "I'll have to hold hearings and I'll criticize what you've done, but don't worry about it. You're doing the right thing."

When I spoke to Regan I told him I was exhausted and would like to leave the FDIC as soon as he could find a replacement.

He said, "You just need a vacation. Take some time off, and don't make any decisions now. We can't get a new person in the job until after the election in November, so you've got time to think about what you want to do. I'd like to see you reappointed after the election."

I promised I would think about it.

It was July 26, 1984, and we were ready to take the assistance plan to the FDIC board and announce it. I was emotionally and physically drained. After the board approved the plan, I tried to thank the FDIC staff for all they had done.

I began, "I want to say one more thing before we adjourn."

Just then I looked at Doug Jones. My mind flashed back to a recent Sunday evening when Doug came into my office to ask me something. Doug is one of the clearest thinkers I know, but he was making no sense that evening. He was exhausted and was almost babbling. I remembered the guy who headed the FDIC effort at Penn Square who was nearly incoherent over the phone just before being hospitalized for exhaustion. I said, "Doug, go home. You're making no sense. Go home and get some sleep." He protested, but I insisted.

Looking at Doug in the boardroom, I was overcome with emotion. I was so thankful for the extraordinary efforts throughout the past several years by the FDIC staff. And I was so relieved Continental was coming to closure.

Tears started to come and I said, "I'm sorry . . . I can't . . . the meeting's adjourned."

I rushed to my office and tried to pull myself together. I had to go upstairs in a few minutes to face the press to announce the Continental package and respond to questions. I did not have an ounce of energy left and did not see how I could pull it off.

When I entered the room upstairs, it was jammed with reporters and TV cameras. Neither the FDIC nor I was used to such a scene. I do not know how or where I got it, but a burst of energy flowed into me. The press conference could not have gone better.

The rescue package was well received in the marketplace. Continental's funding situation improved steadily. The company was able to pay off its borrowings from the Fed and turn a profit much sooner than projected.

■ ■ ■

A couple of months after the announcement, I got a big scare. Swearingen and Ogden had been battling constantly. I received calls periodically from one or the other asking who was in charge of Continental. I would ask why they needed to know. Were they having some policy disagreement? After determining they had no specific problem or issue, I would suggest that we leave the issue of who was in charge for another day.

On this day, it was Swearingen who called. He was tired of not knowing who was in charge and he was going to convene a special board meeting to resolve the issue. I was aghast. Continental was far from out of the woods. Swearingen and Ogden having a shoot-out at a special board meeting would almost certainly leak and be widely reported in the press. It was easy to visualize Continental's funding drying up again. I asked Swearingen if there was any particular problem or disagreement.

"No," he responded, "I just want to settle the question of who's in charge."

I said, "John, you can't call a special board meeting. It'll be all over the press, and the bank might not survive it."

"It's too late. I've already done it," he replied firmly.

I pleaded with him to cancel the board meeting. I promised to come to Chicago personally to help resolve the issue. I said we would meet secretly with a few key directors to work out something. He again refused.

Finally, I said. "John, I can't let you convene the board to resolve this issue. I'll have to take action."

He responded gruffly, "Do whatever you have to do. I'm not canceling the meeting."

I got more direct, "John, you're telling your 80 percent shareholder to stick it up his ass, and I can't let you do that. I'll have to replace you. Please think about it, and we'll talk later."

To which he responded, "We can talk later, but I'm not changing my mind. I'm going to get this issue decided."

We would have to replace Swearingen if he did not back down, and it did not appear likely he would. He had made up his mind and there was no dissuading him.

I asked Jack Murphy—the FDIC's new general counsel who had come in from the Cleary Gottlieb firm—if we had authority to fire Swearingen. It was doubtful. Continental's board would have to do it, and it was not clear whether the directors would side with the FDIC or Swearingen. The FDIC had already informed most of the directors that they would not be allowed to continue on the board. We had some clout with them, though, because they could be sued by the FDIC for Continental's demise.

If we were going to fire Swearingen, we would need to find a replacement of considerable stature. I called Tony Solomon, who had recently retired as president of the Federal Reserve Bank of New York. Prior to holding that position he had been a successful businessman and had held a senior position at Treasury. I reached him in Palm Springs, where ironically he had a home near Swearingen's.

I told Tony about the dispute with Swearingen and asked if he would be willing to serve as nonexecutive chairman of Continental if I had to fire Swearingen. He said he would and we agreed on a compensation package over the phone.

Jack Murphy and I decided I should call Swearingen to see whether he would go quietly or fight us.

I began, "John, I'm having a press release drafted to announce your departure. Do you want it to say that you're being fired or that you've resigned?"

"Well, I guess it would be better to say I've resigned," Swearingen replied.

I agreed and expressed my regret, although I breathed a quiet sigh of relief that he was going to go without a fight. I reiterated that I would be willing to come to Chicago to work things out if he canceled the board meeting. I sensed no softening of his position.

I shifted gears, "Before I hang up, John, do you want to know who your successor is?"

He allowed that he did.

"I believe you know him," I said, "It is Tony Solomon."

Swearingen paused for what seemed like a long time.

Finally he said, "He's a good man."

Another long pause—then he added, "Did you say you'd be willing to meet with a few directors to work this out?"

Swearingen was a tough oilman, used to getting his way. He also knew when to fold and that time was at hand. I told him I would come to Chicago soon and we would have a private meeting with some key directors.

I added, "Does this mean you're going to cancel the special board meeting?"

He promised he would.

A week or so later, I flew to Chicago and met in a private room at the O'Hare Hilton with Swearingen, Ogden, and four directors who were going to remain on the board.

I opened the meeting, explaining its purpose. I said neither man would have taken his job if he had known he was going to be junior to the other, so we had worked out a deal to make them equal. Unfortunately, neither was willing to continue that way, so we needed to decide who was boss.

I concluded, "I could dictate the answer, but I don't believe that would be appropriate. If this company's ever going to be accepted in the marketplace again, its board of directors, not the FDIC, will need to be in control. So I'm here today as a facilitator and observer. I'll abide by whatever you work out."

It quickly became obvious there was little support for Ogden. He tried to make his case, but his arguments were falling on deaf ears. Mr. Swearingen—Mr. Chicago—had the home field advantage. After an hour or so, I asked Ogden if I could talk with him. We went into the hallway, and I told him he was fighting a lost cause.

He said, "What do you advise me to do?"

"I wouldn't blame you if you resigned," I answered. "You told me you wouldn't accept the job if you had to report to Swearingen, and the deal's being changed on you. But I don't believe the bank can make it if you resign now. I hope you'll stay on for a year or so. Maybe you'll win over the board. If not, your resignation a year from now will cause far less damage."

To his everlasting credit, Ogden went back into the room and said he would accept the decision and remain at the bank for the foreseeable future. He and Swearingen never made their peace. When Swearingen retired a couple of years later, Ogden left and Tom Theobald was brought in to run Continental.

■■■

In the current debate about what is "too big to fail," the term is loosely defined or not defined at all. What does it mean? Did Continental fail or was it bailed out? What would have happened if we had not rescued Continental? Should we allow future Continental-type rescues?

My view is that Continental was "too big to liquidate," but was allowed to fail in most important ways. Shareholders ultimately lost everything and we replaced senior management and most directors. The FDIC took significant control over the direction of the institution and ordered Continental to shrink its balance sheet by 50 percent within three years. What we did not do is destabilize the financial system by imposing losses on Continental's creditors.

I am a huge proponent of free markets and believe the markets should be encouraged to discipline errant behavior by financial institutions. That is why I argued so forcefully that Penn Square should be liquidated and that SeaFirst, Continental Illinois, and the other banks involved should be allowed to feel the pain of their actions at Penn Square.

But there is a time and place for everything. Using good judgment in deciding what to do in different climates is critical in bank supervision and crisis control.

A very large bank could be allowed to fail in isolation. The problem is that very large banks seldom, if ever, get into trouble in isolation. The circumstances that bring one large bank to its knees are almost always having a similar impact on the other large players.

I have no doubt at all that if we had liquidated Continental Illinois, chaos would have ensued throughout the worldwide financial system. First Chicago, Manufacturers Hanover, Chemical Bank, Bank of America, Chase Manhattan Bank, all of the major Texas and Oklahoma banks, and all of the major S&Ls, including the FSLIC, would have been in imminent danger of failing. Widespread panic would have been unavoidable. We almost certainly would have been forced to nationalize the major banks.

It was not just that Continental Illinois was large. It was not just that Continental was *interconnected* (to use today's buzzword, which is almost as overused as *transparency*) to other financial institutions. Those elements were part of the equation. The real issue was that if we had allowed Continental Illinois to fail and be liquidated, we would have triggered a *panic*, which is precisely what happened when the government allowed Lehman Brothers to file for bankruptcy in 2008.

Managing a crisis is more art than science—it requires a good deal of judgment about how much disruption and uncertainty the public psyche can tolerate. I will go into more detail later, but it is clear to me that our management (or mismanagement) of the crisis of 2008 took the public past the tipping point.

Those who argue, as many pundits and politicians are doing in the aftermath of the crisis of 2008, that "too big to fail" must be eradicated and that the powers of the Fed and FDIC to act decisively to stop a conflagration in the financial system must be weakened or even eliminated are terribly misguided. We must not impede the authority of these two agencies to prevent panic in the banking system—that, after all, is their raison d'être.

Chapter 8

Preparing to Leave

President Reagan was reelected in November 1984 and I called Treasury Secretary Regan a few days later. I reminded him that I had promised to reconsider leaving the FDIC and that we had agreed to talk after the election. I said it was time for me to return to the private sector and asked that he begin the search for my successor. I agreed to remain in place until the Senate confirmed my successor. I did not realize it would be another year before I could leave.

Most of my final year was spent getting the agency prepared for the future. Bank failures were climbing with no end in sight. We made plans for handling the failures of most of the major banks in the Southwest.

I asked the staff to develop a contingency plan for dealing with the failure in a single year of 200 community banks plus the more or less simultaneous failure of three large regional banks and one or more money center banks. When I asked a senior person in the liquidation division, Mike Hovan, to head the planning exercise he seemed annoyed because he was overwhelmed with handling the bank failures that had already occurred or were imminent.

I said, "Mike, humor me and get this done, as I am afraid it's not a hypothetical exercise."

We finished 1985 with 120 failures and broke through the 200 barrier in 1987, with virtually every large bank in Texas and Oklahoma failing. When Congress finally addressed the S&L crisis in 1989, it merged the FSLIC into the FDIC and the FDIC handled 534 bank and thrift failures that year.

We developed a contingency plan for handling the failure of the largest banks in the country in the event of a default by one or more of the less-developed countries. The situation could turn into a disaster of immense proportions if they not only defaulted, but also renounced their debts. We would have had no choice but to nationalize the major banks.

We also conducted an FDIC study of the S&L industry and the inability of the FSLIC to cope with the problems. We concluded cleaning up the mess would require some $15 billion more than the FSLIC had, and the problems would only get worse over time. I hand delivered the study to Jim Baker, who had replaced Don Regan as secretary of the Treasury (Regan had become chief of staff to the president). As far as I know, Baker did nothing with it.

The FDIC's staff was growing at a breakneck pace. We recognized the need to build a new facility in the Washington area to serve as a training center for personnel from the FDIC and other state and federal bank regulators. Any time an agency builds a new building there is a risk of attracting criticism. I decided to forge ahead on this project to spare my successor from the heat. Imagine my dismay when, at the dedication ceremony after I left the FDIC, my successor commented on the expensive project he inherited, which is named the "L. William Seidman Center." No good deed goes unpunished.

■■■

I was destined to become embroiled in one more controversy before I left the FDIC—this time with the General Accounting Office (now known by the oxymoron, *Government Accountability Office*). Congress established the GAO in 1921 to audit the books of government agencies. It has grown enormously over the years and boasts more than 3,500 employees operating from offices throughout the country and abroad. Its annual budget exceeds $500 million.

Early in my chairmanship, the GAO asked the FDIC to open its problem bank files to GAO personnel who were conducting a study of the effectiveness of bank supervision. I instructed the staff to turn them down.

The GAO requested a meeting with me. They said it was important that they be given access to our files. I said I did not trust them to keep the material confidential. I added that I did not see any purpose to be served since the GAO was not qualified to determine if the FDIC was doing a good, bad, or indifferent job supervising banks.

They did not take kindly to my comments and threatened to get a congressional subpoena. I said they were welcome to try, but even if they got the subpoena, they were not going to be given access to the FDIC files.

I never heard back from them. I do not know if they tried to get a subpoena and could not. More likely, the study they were doing was not authorized by Congress, as my sense is that many of the studies the GAO undertakes are self-initiated projects that it persuades some member of Congress to officially request.

Early in 1985, after the Continental Illinois rescue effort, the GAO came visiting again. They said they could not sign off on the FDIC's year-end financial statements unless we established a reserve for losses at Continental.

I explained that we were not ready to establish a reserve. It would take several months of additional analysis of the loans acquired from Continental before we could be comfortable establishing a reserve for losses. We were sensitive about putting out bad numbers because of the way the Continental deal was structured. The old shareholders of Continental Illinois might have their ownership diminished or even wiped out, depending on the FDIC's losses. Thus, any loss estimate published by the FDIC would have a direct impact on the market price of the shares held by the old shareholders of Continental.

I told the GAO it should include a footnote in the FDIC's statements saying that the FDIC had not provided for losses at Continental and the omission could have a material impact on the FDIC's financial condition. That was not good enough for them.

They threatened that they would not certify the FDIC's statements without a reserve for losses at Continental. I replied that the FDIC did not care if they did not certify the statements.

Next came a congressional hearing asking me to explain why I was not cooperating with the GAO. I provided my reasoning and took some verbal abuse, but we still did not provide a reserve number for Continental Illinois.

■■■

That was where things stood when I left the FDIC at the end of 1985. My successor, Bill Seidman (whose accounting firm is today BDO Seidman), decided to make peace with the GAO. The GAO required the FDIC to restate its financial statements for 1984 to reflect a $1.8 billion reserve for losses at Continental.

I was astounded when I heard about it. When we did the Continental transaction, we estimated our best case as break-even and our worst case as a $1 billion loss. Several years later, when the FDIC's involvement at Continental was finally over, the FDIC's actual losses totaled $1.1 billion. The reserve for losses established by the GAO was overstated by $700 million. That is not close, even for government work.

I could rest my case on the competence of the GAO in regard to its dealings with the FDIC, but it should not be let off the hook so easily. Fast-forward a few years to the belated recognition and cleanup of the S&L crisis in 1989.

Embarrassed by the failure to deal sooner with the S&L debacle, Congress granted the GAO authority to establish loss reserves for the FDIC. The GAO began requiring the FDIC to reserve for losses not only on banks that had already failed (the FDIC's traditional practice), but also for losses on banks that had not failed but might.

Never mind that the FDIC could not determine with accuracy which banks were going to fail, much less the loss the FDIC would suffer if they did. The GAO required the FDIC to make these estimates to the GAO's satisfaction.

The FDIC's future income stream is entirely predictable. It has the power to tax banks whatever amount it needs to cover losses. The GAO gave the FDIC no credit for its future income, while making it reserve for highly speculative losses on future failures.

The result was that the GAO required the FDIC in the early 1990s to create a reserve for losses that was overstated by $8 billion. The FDIC fund was reported to the public as being insolvent by some $7 billion, when in fact it was never insolvent.

Banks were failing left and right and refusing to lend money. Tough times were made even tougher when the FDIC was required to tax banks an extra $8 billion to cover nonexistent losses—all courtesy of Congress and the GAO.

■■■

This problem continues today and the numbers are much larger. In late 2009, the FDIC was showing that its fund, which stood at $50 billion going into the crisis of 2008, had turned negative. As a result, the FDIC required the banks to accelerate their payment of the next three years' premiums (roughly $45 billion) to alleviate concerns about the fund.

The great bulk of the $50 billion–plus nominal decline in the FDIC fund is accounted for by reserves required by the GAO on past failures and future failures that may never occur. I would bet dinner in a fancy restaurant that the FDIC's reserves for losses are significantly overstated, based on the failures that have already occurred and those we believe are likely to occur.

Overstating the FDIC's reserves has significant costs. It drains the banking system of capital and lending capacity at the worst possible time, and it raises public alarm about the FDIC's ability to cope with problems.

Chapter 9

Lessons Learned

My years at the FDIC were enormously fulfilling. I am convinced that had we not handled the banking problems very well, we would have suffered problems more severe than those encountered in the 1930s. The 1930s involved thousands of small bank failures, while the 1980s involved banks of all sizes, including many of the largest. I enjoyed going to work each morning with the feeling that we were making a big difference in people's lives.

I have never worked with a more dedicated group of employees than I did while at the FDIC. The FDIC's employees work tirelessly and are committed to serving the public interest. It was a very sad day for me when I left the agency in late 1985. The job had taken a toll on my personal life and the financial sacrifice was significant, so I needed to move on, albeit with much regret.

We did not accomplish all we had hoped or set out to do. Losing the battle with the money brokers was a bitter pill. Not being able to persuade the public that the S&L crisis was serious and getting worse by the day was a huge disappointment. Having Continental Illinois fail and disrupt our efforts to reform the deposit insurance system was really unfortunate.

My years as chairman of the FDIC were filled with controversy. I did not seek the controversy—it came with running the FDIC in a very difficult period. To do my job properly, I could not help but offend one group or another on almost any important decision. All I could do is what I thought to be in the public interest and let the record speak for itself over time.

■■■

I was then and am today a proponent of free markets. I supported the prompt removal of government-imposed restrictions on competition, such as interest rate controls and limitations on geographic expansion. These restrictions were hurting financial institutions and their customers. There were many vested interests in the status quo, and change is frightening to many people. Many banks, thrifts, community groups, and bank competitors fought deregulation every step of the way.

For deregulation to be successful, the quality of bank supervision needed to be improved greatly. A deregulated financial system is faster moving and more complex. I supported strengthening the examination and enforcement capabilities of the FDIC and the other bank regulators. Many bankers objected, as did the other agencies when they thought the FDIC was encroaching on their turf.

When I arrived at the FDIC in 1978, most of the major banks had tangible equity capital to assets in the 3 percent range with a couple below that number. The FDIC felt strongly that no bank, no matter how seemingly good, should be allowed to go below 5 percent tangible equity to assets. I remember well arguments with the Comptroller's Office, and to a lesser extent with the Fed, in which they took the position that capital was irrelevant in large banks—all that really mattered was liquidity. This was actually similar to the argument that the Treasury made a few years later about the S&L industry—it was not a capital problem but a liquidity problem. The argument was wrongheaded, but it continued 20 years later in the context of the Basel II international capital rules, which I discuss later.

I believed the government could not tell banks they were free to do whatever they needed to do to compete in the marketplace and then bail out their creditors when the banks got into trouble. The scope of the deposit insurance system had to be curtailed. We worked hard to bring that about. We advocated deposit insurance reforms, and we invented new ways to handle bank failures, such as the modified payoff, to impose greater discipline without causing undue disruption for uninsured depositors. We attempted to shut down the massive abuse of the deposit insurance system by money brokers, only to be stymied by a terrible court decision and a Congress pandering to the big money interests.

If creditors were going to be put at greater risk in banks, we needed to improve financial disclosures by banks. We took a number of steps to do precisely that, including advocating that enforcement actions be disclosed, which is now done routinely. I also argued for disclosure of the regulators' confidential bank ratings, but dropped that idea after I became convinced it would do considerable damage to the bank examination process.

The untimely demise of Continental Illinois, and our decision to rescue it, made it untenable for us to continue our efforts to impose greater losses on depositors. The deposit insurance system had been bailing out too many creditors of too many large banks for too long. The banking system had become hooked on deposit insurance and was very troubled and fragile. We believed the financial system could not withstand that much change that abruptly.

■ ■ ■

One common mistake I have witnessed among political appointees at government agencies is a seemingly irresistible urge to make the correct political decision. Adopting a rigorous program to contain the savings bank problems as the industry was struggling with extraordinarily high interest rates was anything but popular. It proved to be the absolutely right policy, though, when measured by the $2 billion cost of cleaning up the savings bank problems versus the nearly $150 billion cost of cleaning up the S&L problems.

Politically, it was almost foolhardy to take on the massive abuses of the deposit insurance system by the enormously powerful money brokers. We did not win that battle, but I firmly believe it was a battle worth fighting. If we had won, taxpayers would have been spared tens of billions of dollars of losses in the S&L industry.

It never occurred to me to worry about whether it would be politically correct to let Penn Square fail or to rescue Continental Illinois. I believe both decisions were made for the right reasons in the context of their time.

Another mistake public leaders sometimes make is being too rigid in their thought process, seeing things too simply or in black and white terms. Having core principles and being centered is important but so is using judgment and being nuanced.

I believe strongly that free markets, democracy, and economic prosperity go hand in hand. My belief in free markets leads me to dislike government restrictions on competition. My understanding of human nature and my life's experience lead me to support stronger and smarter prudential supervision of deregulated firms and to seek ways to impose greater marketplace discipline.

The same guy who fought hard over the July Fourth weekend in 1982 to let Penn Square Bank fail in order to impose greater marketplace discipline also told the senior deputy Comptroller of the Currency that same weekend that we would stop the contagion at SeaFirst and Continental Illinois—and then delivered on that promise.

Good bank regulation always leans against the prevailing wind. When everything is bright and rosy and bankers and others begin to believe that the business cycle has been repealed, a regulator should be searching hard for potential problems and cautioning banks to slow their growth and build their capital and reserves. When things turn dark and everyone believes the sky is falling, a regulator should encourage bankers to work with their borrowers whenever possible. Bank regulations and bank regulators should always operate in a countercyclical manner.

Bank regulators, and the FDIC in particular, have a lot of priorities, some of which are in conflict at times. Regulators are concerned about bank soundness, ensuring compliance with laws and regulations, minimizing risks to taxpayers, promoting economic growth, protecting bank shareholders and creditors while maintaining market discipline, ensuring that bank customers are treated fairly, and maintaining public confidence in the system.

When it is crunch time and the system is threatened, one priority must take precedence over all others—maintaining public confidence in the system. I believe we took care of that top priority in the 1980s, which allowed us to handle some 3,000 bank and thrift failures, including many very large firms, without panicking the public or the financial markets. I believe the failure in 2008 to take care of that top priority led to a panic in the financial markets, which in turn led to a much deeper recession and more banking problems than would have otherwise occurred.

After I left the FDIC at the end of 1985 there was still a lot of cleaning up to do in the banking industry, the most immediate and notable problems being in the southwestern states of Texas and Oklahoma where nearly every large bank ultimately failed. A rolling real estate recession went from the Southwest to the West Coast, to the Southeast and finally to the Northeast and Mid-Atlantic states, wiping out regional banks and community banks and thrifts along its path.

The first Bush Administration and Congress finally decided to clean up the festering S&L mess in 1989, five years after I told Treasury Secretary Jim Baker that it was the top issue in the financial system. The defunct FSLIC was folded into the FDIC and the Resolution Trust Corporation (RTC) was created, under the FDIC's oversight, to dispose of the assets of failed S&Ls. Taxpayers lost nearly $150 billion.

I cringe when I think about how much more cheaply the problems could have been handled five years earlier when I gave Secretary Baker the FDIC's study of the S&L industry. I fume when I think about how much money Wall Street firms made helping to create the problems and then helping to clean them up.

■■■

My successor, Bill Seidman, and I got off to a rocky start. I am not sure why, because I could not have extended myself to him any more completely. I let him use my conference room as his office for a couple of months while he awaited Senate confirmation and gave him complete access to all FDIC personnel and files.

My guess is that he thought I was a bit toxic after all of the controversy I had stirred up, and he wanted to distance himself from me and make peace with the Treasury, the GAO, the money brokers, and anyone else who had a complaint about something I had done or not done. It took him maybe a year or two to become even more controversial than I, including engaging in open warfare with the other banking agencies and White House chief of staff John Sununu. It comes with the job when you are running the FDIC in very difficult times.

Bill and I made our peace in later years and became allies on any number of issues, including our opposition to the Basel II capital accords and mark-to-market accounting. The last time I saw him was a little over a month before his death in May 2009 when he and I were asked to attend an informal Democratic leadership meeting in the conference room of House Majority Leader Steny Hoyer to discuss the financial crisis and the economy. I do not believe that Bill and I differed on any issue, and I am glad I got to see him one last time. He was a good man who dedicated a substantial portion of his life to public service.

The other major figure handling the banking crisis of the 1980s was Paul Volcker. Paul and I had our battles while in our respective roles, but there is no person in public service I respect more than him. We have stayed in touch in the years since and occasionally talk by telephone or have lunch or dinner in New York City. He came to my farewell party when I left the FDIC, and I presented him an XXXL FDIC nylon jacket, which he assures me he uses for fishing outings. I was quite moved 18 years after I left the FDIC when Paul attended and said some very kind words at my surprise sixtieth birthday party.

Part Two

HERE WE GO AGAIN

Chapter 10

Policy Mistakes—1989 through 2007

I absolutely believe that we drew the wrong lessons from crisis of the 1980s, particularly the S&L crisis, and adopted the wrong reforms, which led to the crisis of 2008 and 2009. This conclusion is not based on 20-20 hindsight. I and others have been cautioning for the past two decades that we would live to regret many of the reforms being made.

The causes of the S&L crisis were straightforward and clear to those who had more than passing knowledge of it. Thrifts were created more than a century ago as mutual (nonstock) organizations to help working families pool their money to purchase homes. At the time, banks were focused on business lending and did not cater to consumers.

By the 1970s, a whole lot had changed in the financial world, but S&Ls were stuck in a time warp. They were still taking consumer deposits and investing them in long-term, fixed-rate mortgages and government bonds. Government regulation of deposit interest rates imposed in the 1930s was still in effect and S&Ls were allowed to pay one-quarter percent higher than banks, which had moved heavily into consumer deposits and loans, including mortgages.

The Nixon Administration created a task force in the early 1970s (the Hunt Commission) that recommended that S&Ls be allowed to become more banklike in their activities. The recommended reforms made a lot of sense but were not feasible politically so the S&Ls remained stuck in an increasingly uneconomic business model.

Inflation careened out of control and interest rates shot to 21.5 percent in 1979. Thrifts suffered a grievous blow. Depositors fled to the newly developed mutual funds and money market funds, commercial paper, and government securities so they could get much higher rates of interest than thrifts were allowed to pay.

The government deregulated interest rate controls as quickly as possible to help banks and thrifts to maintain their funding (I was a member of the Depository Institutions Deregulation Committee, which oversaw the deregulation of interest rates). But the squeeze on profits was enormous as the thrifts had to pay much higher deposit interest rates but could not increase the interest they were receiving on their holdings of long-term, fixed-rate mortgages and government securities. They were hemorrhaging red ink and their capital was being depleted at an alarming rate. Virtually the entire industry was in serious danger of collapsing.

■■■

The FDIC had the same issues with the savings bank industry that the Federal Home Loan Bank Board and FSLIC had with the S&L industry, and the two industries were roughly the same size with the same kinds of portfolios. But the two agencies adopted very different policies in overseeing the two industries, as discussed in Chapter 3.

The Bank Board/FSLIC viewed the S&L problems as being primarily lack of earnings power and lack of liquidity. It was not particularly concerned about the weak management and lack of capital. This view was strongly supported by the Reagan Administration, most state regulators, and the Congress.

They believed that the proper solution was for the S&Ls to grow their way out of the problems. S&Ls were authorized to offer variable rate mortgages and engage in a broader range of lending and business activities. To buy more time for the transition, weak S&Ls were merged together and were allowed to book large amounts of goodwill to artificially bolster their capital. Failing S&Ls were sold to real estate developers and others with little or no banking background or experience in a regulated industry.

A large number of S&Ls grew by leaps and bounds with inadequate management and little or no capital at risk. Heads I win, and tails the government loses. It was a prescription for disaster and that is precisely what we got. The approach was highly politicized and we got the results one would expect from a political solution.

The FDIC pursued a more orthodox and conservative supervisory approach with the savings banks. The savings banks were allowed time to solve their problems, as we felt the problems could be resolved more cheaply once interest rates returned to more normal levels. We told the weak savings banks that they could not grow, could not engage in new activities, and could not increase their risk profile. If they did any of those things, they would be closed immediately.

When a savings bank's capital approached zero (or when depositors began to flee in big numbers), we merged the failing savings bank into a much stronger bank and provided real FDIC financial assistance to ensure the resulting firm would be viable.

We did not want to create a larger problem that would come back to haunt us. We did not engage in regulatory accounting and did not mask the problems. The end result was about $2 billion of losses to the FDIC versus nearly $150 billion in taxpayer losses for the S&Ls.

■■■

Congress and others went into a tizzy over the taxpayer losses in the S&L industry and myriad reforms were made that helped lead us to the current crisis. They believed the regulatory and accounting systems let us down. In reality our government let us down.

Our government refused to reform the S&L industry at a time when it could have done so without major trauma. Our government let inflation get out of control, which brought us 21.5 percent interest rates and nearly collapsed the entire financial system. And our government made a conscious decision not to face up to the S&L crisis and instead to mask the problems and pursue a highly risky strategy of allowing firms with weak management and little or no capital to grow with reckless abandon. These government actions and failures to act did not represent a breakdown in the regulatory and accounting systems, but a widespread failure of our government to protect its citizens from an economic abyss.

Just as government policy mistakes led to and greatly exacerbated the S&L crisis of the 1980s, policy mistakes in the 1990s and the 2000s contributed heavily to the panic of 2008. As you consider the following, ask yourself: *How much worse would the banking and economic crisis of the 1980s have been had these policies been adopted before the 1980s rather than after? If these policies had been in place, how could we have dealt with the prime rate soaring to 21.5 percent, a 2.5 year recession with unemployment hitting almost 11 percent, the massive insolvency of the thrift industry, the bursting of the bubble in the energy sector, a depression in the agricultural sector, a rolling real estate recession that wiped out major regional banks throughout the country, the failure of some 3,000 banks and thrifts, and the insolvency on a market value basis of virtually all of the country's largest banks because of massive investments in real estate and Third World debt?*

If a comparatively small and focused set of problems—primarily subprime mortgage lending—triggered a worldwide panic and deep recession in 2008, how could we have avoided a complete collapse during the 1980s with these policies in place? Finally, ask yourself whether the reforms being debated in Congress in early 2010 would correct the policy mistakes highlighted in this chapter?

Mark-to-Market Accounting

The story of the policy mistakes in the two decades between the crisis of the 1980s and the crisis of 2008 begins with the Securities and Exchange Commission and the Financial Accounting Standards Board (FASB), which sets accounting rules subject to the SEC's oversight. As I discuss in more detail later, the SEC and FASB decided incorrectly that the S&L crisis was caused in significant part by accounting rules, so they decided to impose on the financial industry mark-to-market accounting rules similar to those that had been discredited and abandoned during the Great Depression.

Simply put, mark-to-market accounting requires banks to mark financial assets to whatever price they are worth on any given day. It produces a great deal of volatility and is a highly inappropriate way to determine the value of loans or other long-term assets. It is highly procyclical, meaning it exaggerates market swings, whether up or down. The move to mark-to-market accounting rules was, without question, a very significant contributor to the panic of 2008 and ensuing severe recession.

The sad thing is that these very bad accounting rules were instituted as a result of a serious misdiagnosis of what went wrong in the S&L industry. No accounting system can work when the Administration, the Congress, and the regulators make a conscious decision to subvert it, as they did in handling the S&L problems.

Virtually everyone knew that the entire S&L industry was badly insolvent, but government leaders did not want to deal with it. The Treasury argued that the S&L problem was not a "solvency" problem but a "liquidity and earnings" problem—the S&Ls just needed broader powers and more time so they could grow their way out of their problems by amassing new, higher-yielding assets to offset their older, lower-yielding assets. It was the height of folly.

The FDIC did not resort to accounting gimmicks to mask the savings bank problems despite considerable pressure to do so. It applied instead historical cost accounting as it was intended to be applied, and resolved the problems in an orderly way at a reasonable cost. The accounting system was not broken and did not need to be fixed.

Deposit Insurance Premiums

Congress got it wrong on deposit insurance premiums, which are also administered in a highly procyclical manner. Banks are not required to pay FDIC premiums when times are good, the FDIC fund is flush with money, and bank earnings are strong. When times are tough and the FDIC fund is under a lot of strain, as was the case in much of 2008 and 2009, banks are hit with extraordinary FDIC premiums when they can least afford them. The result is that banks are drained of capital when they most need the capital to cover losses and support new loans.

Prompt Corrective Action

Because Congress viewed the S&L crisis as a product of poor regulatory supervision, it adopted rigid rules (called Prompt

Corrective Action) requiring regulators to take increasingly harsh regulatory actions when a bank's capital falls below certain levels. It sounds good in theory and in normal times it is not a big problem. But when a crisis hits, it denies regulators the ability to use judgment as they did in guiding us through the minefield of the banking crisis of the 1980s. When Prompt Corrective Action is coupled with mark-to-market accounting and procyclical capital and loan loss reserve policies, it becomes particularly counterproductive.

The burden of Prompt Corrective Action falls most heavily on community banks that are deemed "too small to save." After a couple of large bank failures in 2008 (IndyMac and Washington Mutual), the government decided that the financial system could stomach no more. Prompt Corrective Action was put on hold for the largest banks, while small banks continued to feel its full force.

Mathematical Capital Models

Bank regulators added fuel to the procyclical fire when they adopted the Basel Capital Accords (named for the town in Switzerland where the Bank for International Settlements is located). The Basel capital rules apply to large banks throughout the world and are based on highly complex mathematical models that predict the future on the basis of past experience.

You do not have to be a mathematician to know that a model that predicts the future on the basis of the past will have a procyclical bias. If we are in a period of prosperity, backward-looking models tell us that losses are low and banks do not need much capital. This fuels and prolongs the economic boom because banks have plenty of capital to support more lending. If we are in a recession, the models tell us that losses are extraordinarily high and banks need much more capital. This deepens and prolongs the economic slump because banks do not have capital to support new lending. When these capital models are combined with mark-to-market accounting, they produce a procyclical tidal wave.

Loan Securitization

Securitization is used primarily for home mortgages and credit card loans. In its essence, a bank packages the loans into a trust and then sells interests in the trust to investors throughout the world. The securitization markets mushroomed during the 1990s and 2000s and trillions of dollars of assets were removed from the books of banks for purposes of computing capital adequacy.

I have never been comfortable with the accounting treatment that says once these loans are securitized the bank is no longer the owner of them and does not have to maintain capital against them. The reality is that banks must stand behind securitizations and ensure that investors do not lose money if the banks wish to create and market new securitizations—securitizations are not one-time events. Securitizations should be treated as secured borrowings by banks and should be kept on the books for purposes of computing capital requirements.

Allowing securitizations to be removed from the balance sheets (and thus capital requirements) of banks and Wall Street firms created a huge boom in credit card and mortgage loans. We are talking about trillions of dollars of additional leverage in the financial system.

Regulators did little due diligence on the loans when they were in the pipeline because they were destined to be shipped out, and in that process would be rated by the rating agencies (Standard & Poor's, Moody's, and Fitch). The rating agencies, we learned much too late, were not up to the task. Once the loans were securitized, regulators washed their hands of them completely—they had little idea where they went.

Now that we are in the soup, the SEC and FASB are running for cover on securitizations and are creating a procyclical effect in the opposite direction. They have declared that securitizations must be brought back onto bank and Wall Street balance sheets, effective immediately. This requires the financial firms to allocate substantial amounts of capital to the securitizations, which diminishes their ability to make new loans.

While I believe securitizations should not have been allowed off the balance sheets in the first place, I am equally opposed to correcting the problem in one fell swoop in the middle of a serious recession. The SEC and FASB seem to have no concept of the economic harm their accounting pronouncements can create. If they were focused even remotely on the potential consequences of their actions, they would have changed the securitization rules prospectively and allowed the old securitizations to run off. One can only hope that the bank regulators will exhibit better judgment and phase in the capital requirements on the securitizations to help us get out of the recession, although that seems doubtful.

Loan Loss Reserves

The SEC made three additional egregious mistakes to add more procyclicality to the mix. The first was in 1999 when it commenced an enforcement action against SunTrust Bank, charging it with manipulating its earnings (downward) by creating excessive loan loss reserves. This had a chilling effect on loan loss provisioning by banks during the boom years leading up to the crash in 2008. Banks should be building capital and reserves in good times so they are better prepared for the inevitable turn in the economy.

Once we entered the downward cycle and the weaknesses in loan portfolios became evident, banks were required to set aside enormous reserves at a time when they could least afford them. Add this to mark-to-market accounting and procyclical capital models and it becomes extremely difficult for banks to lend enough money to turn around the economy.

Leverage on Wall Street

The SEC's next mistake was to move to Basel-type capital rules in 2004 for investment banking firms regulated by the SEC. Firms such as Bear Stearns and Lehman Brothers tripled their leverage (assets to capital) at the height of the economic boom, with much of the growth coming in real estate lending. No wonder they were among the first to tumble.

Deregulation of Short Sellers

Finally, the SEC in 2007 repealed the Depression-era rules governing short sellers of securities. The uptick rules were put into place in 1938 by then-SEC chairman Joseph P. Kennedy to keep short sellers from unfairly driving down the prices of securities, destabilizing markets, and destroying vast amounts of wealth. The SEC could not have picked a worse time to dismantle the restriction on short sellers—at the height of the economic boom—and the effects were devastating when coupled with mark to market accounting and pro-cyclical regulatory rules.

Repeal of Glass-Steagall

The Glass-Steagall Act is a Depression-era law that separated commercial banking from investment banking. It was enacted for a couple of principal reasons. First, investment banking was considered too risky and volatile for commercial banks that took FDIC-insured deposits from retail depositors and generally operated with higher leverage than investment banks. Second, conflicts of interests between the two lines of business were exposed in the wake of the Great Depression—for example, a bank might sell stock to the public in a company with the proceeds used to pay off a loan to the company that was held by the bank.

The Glass-Steagall restraints were eased over the years until Congress finally repealed them in 1999. I favored repeal because I believed the restrictions were anticompetitive and that regulators could properly supervise the firms and prevent abuses. I now believe that my faith in our ability to properly regulate these highly leveraged and complex firms was misguided.

Repeal of Glass-Steagall, combined with the SEC's substantial easing of capital requirements on investment banking firms, has led to the creation of very large, highly complex, and risky firms. I fear these firms have become too complex to manage or regulate. It is not a coincidence that ground zero for the crisis of 2008 was located in the heart of Wall Street.

Uncontrolled Growth of Freddie and Fannie

Another very important policy mistake setting us up for the panic of 2008 was the breathtaking expansion of Fannie Mae and Freddie Mac, the two mammoth government-sponsored entities charged with expanding home ownership. These agencies were encouraged by both Congress and the Clinton Administration to lower their underwriting standards (for example, by reducing down payment requirements) to allow more lending to lower income borrowers. Their portfolios of mortgage loans held directly and securitized loans skyrocketed from less than one trillion dollars in 1991 to nearly six trillion dollars in 2007.

These two firms increased their leverage enormously at the same time they took on increasingly risky loans to people who could not afford them. Without question, the failure to properly regulate and control Fannie Mae and Freddie Mac was a major factor in creating the crisis of 2008–2009.

Monetary Policy

My focus is on regulatory and accounting issues. Many monetary policy experts believe the Federal Reserve played a large role in the crisis by expanding the money supply much too fast and for much too long to get us out of the recession of 2001 and then putting on the brakes too hard a few years later. Others fault the Fed for not recognizing and deflating the housing bubble in a timely way. While I suspect the critics might have it right, I will stick with the things I know best and let economists debate the role monetary policy may have played in creating the crisis.

Chapter 11

The Subprime Mortgage Problem

Subprime mortgage lending (loans with lower underwriting standards to relatively risky borrowers) is regarded by nearly everyone as a principal cause of the crisis of 2008. The problems became evident in early 2007.

At that time, there was a great deal of concern about potential widespread defaults by borrowers that would lead to massive home foreclosures, failures of financial institutions, a credit crunch in housing, and a recession—with good reason, as it turned out. Congressional committees and the media were wondering how big the problems were, what could be done about them, and whether the bank regulators were doing their jobs properly.

■■■

In terms of how big the problems were, one thing seemed clear—banks and S&Ls, as a whole, did not have major problems with subprime mortgage loans. Most of the problems were associated with Wall Street firms and other nonbank financial institutions.

Bank regulators had been focused on subprime lending for years, and they were reasonably diligent in preventing banks from having undue concentrations of subprime loans. Some banks had indirect exposure to subprime lending because they extended credit to mortgage firms or because they invested in mortgage-backed securities. But it seemed highly unlikely that this would result in unmanageable losses for the banking industry as a whole.

It was difficult to see how the turmoil in subprime mortgage lending could have a significant impact on the economy. It was true that lending standards were about to be raised and that subprime borrowers would have a much harder time gaining access to credit. But if the banks were not in major trouble—and neither I nor the regulators believed they were—the economy would not take much of a hit.

In the fall of 2007, despite the continuing turmoil in the financial markets due to subprime mortgages, I was convinced that the problems were not nearly as severe as some feared and that the biggest fear, as President Roosevelt said when he took office in 1933, was fear itself.

■ ■ ■

In previous downturns, most financial problems were reflected in bank balance sheets. Banks loaned money and for the most part kept the assets on their books. When the economy overheated, the Federal Reserve typically would tighten money, which would raise the cost of borrowing. Banks would cut back on lending, a recession would ensue, and banks would take their lumps.

Regulatory authorities could get a pretty good handle on the dimensions of the problems under those circumstances, because banks were examined regularly and were required to recognize their likely losses based on an analysis of anticipated cash flows. Moreover, because the larger banks were public companies, they were required to publicly disclose their problems.

One interesting thing about the unfolding subprime mortgage crisis in 2007 was that it was not driven by an economic downturn. In the wake of the stock market collapse and the turmoil caused by 9/11, interest rates and the stock market fell precipitously and real estate seemed to be a haven. As the real estate markets heated up, loans were made to investors and other borrowers who had little margin for error, particularly those who used low down payment, adjustable rate mortgages.

The overheated market, led by investors, had to come to an end and it did. The Fed raised interest rates and the rapid escalation in real estate prices came to an abrupt halt in many markets. Investors ran for the exits, creating a giant inventory of housing that would take years to work off in some markets.

It was difficult for investors to assess the dimensions of the subprime mortgage crisis, and the uncertainties were creating significant volatility in the financial markets, especially the market for mortgage-backed securities.

Mortgages are originated by S&Ls, mortgage companies, banks, and others. They are placed into trusts, and securities representing ownership of those trusts (frequently referred to as mortgage-backed securities, or MBS) are sold to investors such as pension funds, hedge funds, banks, and insurance companies.

It is even more complicated than that, as the ownership of the trusts is broken into senior and junior interests. These different types of securities can entail little risk and relatively low yields or high risk and high yields. To make matters worse, investors lost confidence in the rating agencies, which had apparently given strong ratings to securities backed by poorly underwritten loans.

So it is easy to understand why the markets were unnerved and volatile. Markets can handle almost anything, except the lack of accurate information.

■ ■ ■

Another problem with mortgage-backed securities was that no one knew exactly who owned them. But it seemed clear at the time that subprime mortgages were not infecting the banking system to a significant degree.

Inside Mortgage Finance estimates that total subprime mortgage loans outstanding at year-end 2006 stood at $1.24 trillion. Bank regulators estimate that only $300 billion was held in FDIC-insured banks. Seventy-five percent of subprime mortgages were performing (and still were in late 2009), which means that only $75 billion of the subprime loans held by FDIC-insured banks and thrifts were in default.

If the $75 billion in nonperforming subprime loans were written down by 50 percent—a pretty severe haircut given the fact that they were secured by real estate—the result would have translated into writeoffs of only $38 billion. If performing subprime loans were written down 25 percent (to account for *potential* problems associated with those), that would create an additional $56 billion writedown for banks and S&Ls. All told, we are talking about a total writedown on subprime loans held by FDIC-insured institutions of less than $100 billion pretax, using aggressive writedown assumptions.

While $100 billion is not pocket change, it is not a big enough number to cripple a banking industry that in 2006 held $12.3 trillion in assets, had total equity capital and reserves of nearly $1.4 trillion, and earned $150 billion after taxes. It would have been painful, but not catastrophic.

Bank regulators estimated in 2007 that a 15 percent pretax loss on the entire $1.24 trillion in subprime loans was a reasonable assumption. This would have been less than $190 billion spread out over time among investors around the world. A loss of this magnitude would have been just a little greater than the impact of a 1 percent decline in the U.S. stock market in 2007.

■■■

The point I am making is that the subprime mortgage crisis appeared manageable, particularly in the context of FDIC-insured banks. How did we let things spin so badly out of control?

Chapter 12

SEC and FASB Blunders

The U.S. economy was in good shape when the subprime mortgage crisis erupted in 2007. Consumer spending, GDP growth, consumer confidence, job creation, and other vital signs of economic health were all positive and inflation and unemployment were low.

Given that setting, how could the federal government have let a manageable situation deteriorate into a full-blown disaster? During the next two years, we would witness a steep rise in unemployment and home foreclosures, a collapse of consumer spending, destruction of the investment banking industry (Bear Stearns, Lehman Brothers, and Merrill Lynch), nationalization of two giant government-sponsored mortgage institutions (Fannie Mae and Freddie Mac) as well as one of the world's largest financial companies (AIG), frozen financial markets throughout the world, and the near-nationalization of some of our largest commercial banks.

Without question, two of the biggest culprits were the SEC and its sidekick, the FASB. The SEC, beginning in the early 1990s, decided to become proactive in encouraging the markets to shape the financial institutions of the future. The SEC decided that markets are always right or at least are much better regulators of financial institutions than government agencies.

■ ■ ■

The architect of this movement was Richard Breeden, a very smart and articulate fellow who served as chairman of the SEC from 1989 to 1993. I first met Richard when he worked for Vice President Bush in the Reagan Administration, and we got to know each other really well when he served as staff director for the Vice President's Task Force on Regulatory Reform, which included the vice president and the heads of 13 financial regulatory agencies. We put together a decent reform proposal, which has been gathering dust since.

When George H. W. Bush was elected president, one of his first priorities was to clean up the S&L mess, and he tapped Richard to lead that effort. The old FSLIC was merged into the FDIC, and the Resolution Trust Corporation or RTC was created to dispose of the assets of the failed S&Ls. With that formidable task accomplished, the president appointed Richard to head the SEC.

I understand and have sympathy for what was motivating Richard. We spent many hours discussing the S&L mess, and he believed the S&L problems would not have gotten so far out of hand had we subjected the institutions to a greater degree of discipline by market forces.

The SEC moved in the early 1990s to involve the market in the regulation of banks and thrifts through the adoption of mark-to-market accounting. Few had even heard of mark-to-market accounting—also referred to as market value or fair value accounting—when the crisis broke out in 2007, much less understood how it worked or why it was bad.

■ ■ ■

There are essentially two kinds of accounting regimes for financial institutions—historical cost accounting and mark-to-market accounting. Historical cost accounting records loans or other investments by banks at their cost (what the bank paid for them) and leaves them at that price unless the bank (or its accountant or regulator) decides that the value of the loan or investment is permanently impaired. For example, the value of a loan is permanently impaired if the borrower can no longer afford to repay the loan on the agreed terms, in which case the loan or investment is written down to it true economic value (based on estimated cash flows). Historical cost accounting never writes up values unless an asset is sold to a third party for more than the bank invested in the asset.

Mark-to-market accounting is horribly complicated. But in its simplest form, financial assets of banks must be continuously marked to market prices. This is not a big deal if markets are in balance and behaving properly. The rub comes when something spooks the markets, as seems to happen every decade or two. When panic selling sets in and markets collapse, mark-to-market accounting requires banks to write down assets and record huge earnings losses that deplete capital. This spooks the markets further, requiring more writedowns. The downward spiral feeds on itself.

Banks need capital to lend. They typically lend about $10 for every dollar of capital. So if mark-to-market accounting requires the writedown of $500 billion of bank capital, as it did in 2008, bank lending capacity is reduced by $5 trillion. The dearth of bank lending ripples throughout the economy and further depresses the markets and economic activity.

Bank regulators had imposed mark-to-market accounting on banks before 1938 with very poor results. In that year, President Roosevelt asked Treasury Secretary Henry Morgenthau to convene bank regulators to determine why the country was mired in an economic depression for eight years. They concluded that mark-to-market accounting was inhibiting bank lending and abolished it in favor of historical cost accounting.

It was against this historical backdrop that the SEC and FASB decided in the 1990s to embark on their crusade to reimpose mark-to-market accounting on the financial system. FDIC Chairman William Taylor, Fed Chairman Alan Greenspan, and Treasury Secretary Nicholas Brady wrote letters to the SEC and FASB reminding them of the history of mark-to-market accounting and its highly procyclical effects and urged the SEC and FASB not to go down that path. Their pleas were ignored. Secretary Brady's March 24, 1992, letter was prescient:

> [Mark-to-market accounting] could result in extremely volatile earnings and capital. This volatility would not be indicative of a bank's operating results and would therefore be misleading to . . . users of financial statements. . . . Moreover, [mark-to-market accounting] could even result in more intense and frequent credit crunches, since a temporary dip in asset prices would result in immediate reductions in bank capital and an inevitable retrenchment in bank lending capacity.

The SEC and FASB were irresponsible to have relentlessly followed a policy that led to the massive and senseless destruction of capital within the U.S. financial system, which had been the envy of the world. They were warned by the heads of the three government agencies responsible for maintaining a sound economy and financial system that mark-to-market accounting would lead to the kind of crisis confronting us in 2008, and they were arrogant enough to charge ahead anyway.

This is contrary to everything we know about prudent bank regulation. When there are temporary impairments of asset values due to economic and marketplace events, regulators must give institutions an opportunity to survive the temporary impairment. Assets should not be marked down to unrealistic fire-sale prices. Regulators must evaluate the assets on the basis of their true economic value (a cash-flow analysis).

If we had followed the mark-to-market approach during the 1980s, we would have nationalized all of the major banks in the country, and thousands of additional banks and thrifts would have failed. I have no doubt that the country would have gone from a serious recession into a widespread depression.

■■■

I campaigned almost nonstop against mark-to-market accounting as the financial crisis deepened in 2008 and 2009. I argued that if we did not halt the insanity of forcing financial firms to mark assets to nonexistent market values instead of their true economic value, the cancer would keep spreading and would plunge the world into very difficult economic times for years to come.

By the fall of 2008, this policy caused the inexcusable destruction of more than $500 billion of capital in our financial system, creating a stifling credit crunch and undermining public confidence in the financial system. Nearly two years later, the effects of the resulting severe credit crunch were still evident. People could not get financing to purchase or renovate homes, and small to medium size businesses were starved for credit.

It is unfathomable that the SEC did not suspend mark-to-market accounting to prevent those adverse consequences. It is equally unfathomable that the Bush and Obama Administrations sat on their hands instead of ordering the regulators to deal with the issue, as President Roosevelt did in 1938. Former Treasury Secretary Henry Paulson bears a large share of the blame, and his successor, Timothy Geithner, has followed in Paulson's footsteps.

When Congress enacted the $700 billion financial bailout legislation in October 2008, provisions were added requiring the SEC to conduct a study of mark-to-market accounting to determine whether it was exacerbating the economic crisis. It was a useless exercise.

It would be refreshing, even confidence building, for the SEC to admit its policies failed. But then-SEC chairman Christopher

Cox made it clear in a speech before the study was concluded that the SEC would do no such thing. He devoted pages to justifying the existing process for setting accounting standards under the mysterious five-member board of accountants called the FASB, which moves at glacial speed when it moves at all.

Cox's words were stunningly brazen, considering the huge mess the SEC had made of the financial system:

> Accounting standards should not be viewed as a fiscal policy tool to stimulate or moderate economic growth, but rather as a means of producing objective measurements of the financial performance of public companies. Accounting standards aren't just another financial rudder to be pulled when the economic ship drifts in the wrong direction. . . .
> It cannot be said often enough that effective standards require a dispassionate arbiter. . . . [A] standard setter must be independent . . . from the political process . . . and from national or regional biases.

His words were divorced from history, facts, and economic reality. The FASB moved to mark-to-market accounting in the early 1990s in response to enormous pressure brought by the SEC—the agency that was claiming in 2008 that the standard setter must be independent "from the political process." The SEC's leadership in the 1990s pushed FASB into adopting mark-to-market accounting on the false premise that the S&L crisis would not have gotten out of hand had S&Ls been required to mark their assets to market values.

The SEC was not trying to improve the clarity of financial statements, it was trying to force banks and S&Ls into a different business model in which they could not afford to hold long-term assets. A fatal flaw in that theory is that our economy depends on banks and S&Ls converting relatively short-term customer deposits into longer-term loans and investments.

Chairman Cox went on about the SEC's mark-to-market accounting study:

> [M]ost investors . . . agree that fair value is a meaningful and transparent measure of an investment for financial reporting purposes. Financial reporting is intended to meet the needs of investors. While financial reporting may serve as a starting point for other users, such as prudential regulators, the information content provided to investors should not be compromised to meet other needs.

This is from the same SEC that prevented banks from creating adequate loan loss reserves in the good times because it might lead to "earnings management"; allowed investment banks to massively increase their leverage in 2004, leading to the collapse of the entire industry; eliminated controls on short sellers that had been in place since the Great Depression; and failed to uncover the largest Ponzi scheme in history (the Madoff scandal) despite being alerted about the scheme by credible sources on multiple occasions over an entire decade.

I wonder if the SEC has spoken to the millions of people whose investments in financial stocks were wiped out by accounting rules that mark banks' investments to severely and temporarily depressed prices. I wonder if the SEC has spoken to the millions of people who have lost their jobs and homes because the SEC's accounting rules have destroyed trillions of dollars of bank lending capacity.

■ ■ ■

The SEC issued its mark-to-market report to Congress on December 30, 2008. As expected, it urged Congress not to suspend mark-to-market accounting standards.

Finally, Congress got fed up with the stonewalling by the SEC and FASB and convened a hearing on March 12, 2009, before the

House Financial Services Subcommittee on Capital Markets. The SEC and FASB were scheduled to testify first, followed by a panel of private citizens, including me. It was a gratifying experience.

I used the opportunity to demonstrate the absurdity of the FASB-SEC position on mark-to-market accounting. I made many of the points I had argued before. But I also provided an example of how ludicrous mark-to-market accounting can be for a major bank, indeed one that was among the 19 largest that received taxpayer money under the TARP program.

This bank held $3.65 billion in mortgage-backed securities as of December 31, 2008. The underlying loans of the mortgage-backed securities were not subprime, but generally quality loans with average seasoning of 17 months, original FICO scores of 749 and original loan-to-value ratios of 73 percent. These are indicators of high quality loans.

The *actual losses* on the $3.65 billion of mortgage-backed securities at year-end 2008 totaled a meager $1.8 million—that is million with an *m*, not billion with a *b*. Also, the maximum expected lifetime losses estimated by the bank totaled only $100 million—again, that is million with an *m*, not billion with a *b*. Yet the FASB-SEC rules on mark-to-market accounting required the bank to write down those mortgage-backed securities by a whopping $913 million!

That is more than nine times the maximum estimated lifetime losses on those mortgage-backed securities. The SEC-FASB mark-to-market rules needlessly destroyed nearly $1 billion of capital in one portfolio of one bank. Multiply that kind of destruction over the entire financial system and you begin to understand just how devastating the impact of mark-to-market accounting was. A reduction of $1 billion in bank capital equates to nearly $10 billion of reduced lending capacity.

Before questioning the witnesses from the SEC and FASB, members of the subcommittee from both parties made opening statements, probably 20 or so in all. With one exception, each member of Congress castigated the SEC and FASB for their intransigence on mark-to-market accounting. Rep. Gary Ackerman (D-N.Y.), urging speedy action, warned the SEC and the FASB that "if you don't act, we will." In his opening statement, Subcommittee Chairman Paul Kanjorski (D-Penn.) said, "If the regulators and standard setters do not act now to improve the standards, then Congress will have to act itself."

The subcommittee told the SEC and FASB to amend their mark-to-market rules by April 2 or else! The FASB did announce a change to the mark-to-market rules on April 2. The FASB maintained that the new rule contains additional factors for judging a significant decrease in market activity for an asset and removes a presumption that all transactions are distressed unless proven otherwise.

To me it was déjà vu all over again. I considered the new FASB proposal to be tepid, at best, and far short of fixing the problems with the FASB-SEC rules on mark-to-market accounting. We still have a lot of work to do. Mark-to-market accounting should be retroactively eliminated except for assets held in trading accounts.

Accounting standards are set by the FASB, a five-member board selected by FASB's trustees (who themselves are selected from trade groups representing the accounting profession). In other words, it is a cozy little secret society. The SEC has authority to overrule the FASB, but almost never does. The result is a system of accounting that is simply not accountable to anyone.

Throughout the ongoing credit crunch and economic crisis, it has been amply clear that Congress needs to create a better system for setting accounting standards. If the FASB remains the standard setter, it should be overseen by a panel consisting of the Federal Reserve, the FDIC, and other agencies that have responsibility for maintaining stability in the financial system and economy. Accounting rules are much too important to be left solely to a board of accountants and an SEC that does not understand the financial system or bank regulation.

Speaking before the Institute of Chartered Accountants in England and Wales on January 21, 2010, Lord Adair Turner, chairman of the Financial Services Authority in England, described the issue quite well and succinctly:

> Banks are different because they matter more, because they can do more harm. That's why we regulate and supervise their business but do not regulate the business of retailers, hoteliers, or manufacturers. That's why there is a special relationship between the banking system and central banks as lenders of last resort. That's why we worry a lot about "too big to fail" considerations. And that's why prudential regulators, central banks, and economic policy makers have a vital interest in the decisions of accounting standard setters on bank accounting standards, which does not apply between regulators and accounting bodies in any other sectors of the economy.

■■■

Mark-to-market accounting was not the only blunder that can be laid at SEC's doorstep. Another issue on which the SEC undermined prudent regulatory policy was on the setting of reserves for loan losses.

You would think that the ground rules for banks maintaining loan loss reserves would be the exclusive purview of the bank regulatory agencies—but not so. The SEC is on the scene, promulgating policies that inhibit bank reserves at the wrong time in the economic cycle. The SEC's policy on this issue, just like mark-to-market accounting, is procyclical when it should be countercyclical.

Back in 1999, the SEC's quest for accounting nirvana led it to bring an enforcement action against SunTrust Bank, alleging that it was manipulating its earnings (downward!) by creating excessive loan loss reserves. The result was that banks could no longer use business judgment in establishing loan loss reserves. They had to develop predictive models based on prior experience, causing reserving policy to become procyclical alongside mark-to-market accounting.

Prevented from creating larger reserves in good economic times, banks showed artificially higher earnings, which they used to increase lending, pay higher dividends, and increase management bonuses. In a serious economic downturn such as 2008 and 2009, the SEC's policies require banks to create ever-higher reserves. This eats heavily into bank profits and capital and inhibits the ability of banks to contribute to an economic recovery through increased lending.

It is extremely important that bank regulation be counter-cyclical, not procyclical. Bank regulatory policy should encourage banks to build loan loss reserves when the economy is strong and the industry is at its most profitable, not when the economy is weak and earnings are down or nonexistent.

The SEC's next mistake was introducing Basel II capital models for investment banking firms in 2004 at the height of the boom. At the time, the elites of the investment banking industry, including the likes of Merrill Lynch, Goldman Sachs, Bear Stearns, and Lehman Brothers, were all subject to regulation by the SEC. The SEC allowed firms such as these to develop their own models for determining how much capital would be appropriate. The result was a massive increase in leverage followed by catastrophic losses.

Having set the table for a disaster of the first order, the SEC threw a bomb in the room by eliminating the uptick rule in 2007. The uptick rule required that a short sale of stock could be made only at a price above the previous transaction in that security. The uptick rule was put into place in 1938 by Joseph P. Kennedy, the first chairman of the SEC, in order to stop abusive short selling transactions that were decimating the markets and impeding an economic recovery.

Another rule designed to prevent abuses by short sellers was the prohibition against naked short sales. The rule prohibited short sales of securities that were not controlled by the short seller. If you could sell securities you did not control and did not have to observe the uptick rule, you could destroy almost any stock and you would not need much money to do it.

Eliminating the uptick rule and failing to properly enforce the naked short sale rule—in combination with introducing mark-to-market accounting, inhibiting loan loss reserves, and reducing capital requirements for investment banks—set the stage for the crisis of 2008, which began on Wall Street and wreaked havoc on Main Streets throughout the world.

The SEC's sidekick, FASB, added even more fuel to the fire when it allowed financial institutions to engage in trillions of dollars of securitizations, swaps, and other activities off their balance sheets during the 1990s and 2000s. This had the effect of increasing leverage in the financial system enormously and reducing the ability of regulators to identify, understand, and control risks. The accounting was opaque at best. It was thought, incorrectly it turns out, that the rating agencies would be able to tell us all we needed to know about the risks in these off-balance-sheet activities.

Now that we all understand the fallacy of this accounting and regulatory approach, the FASB has reacted by requiring banking firms to bring trillions of dollars of these off-balance-sheet instruments back onto their books. While I agree these activities need to be on the books of banks, the FASB and SEC have shown no sensitivity to the macroeconomic impact of their decisions.

We are in the middle of a deep and prolonged recession. We need banks to help lead us to recovery by increasing lending. The FASB and SEC senselessly destroyed $5 trillion of lending capacity through mark-to-market accounting. Now, instead of transitioning to the new rules on securitization prospectively (for example, allowing the old securitizations to simply run off), the FASB has ordered the banks to bring trillions of dollars of old securitizations onto the books immediately. This destroys trillions of dollars more of bank lending capacity and further impedes economic recovery.

■ ■ ■

Despite the SEC's incredibly bad performance on so many fronts during the past two decades, none of the financial reform proposals being seriously considered in Congress addresses how we might reform the SEC to ensure it is a more effective and responsible agency going forward. Nor do they bring the FASB under meaningful government supervision.

Chapter 13

Schizophrenic Failure Resolution

Financial markets and the public can handle almost anything except uncertainty. If they believe they are being told the truth, someone is in charge with a sensible plan for dealing with the problems, and the system is aboveboard and fair, they can accept almost any negative news.

When problems surfaced at major financial institutions in 2008, the government's actions were ad hoc and inconsistent. No one appeared to be in charge with an overall plan, statements were made that proved false, the public was provided inadequate information, and decision making seemed dominated too much by political considerations, and specifically by Wall Street. The markets and the public lost confidence and financial panic swept the world. Conditions got so bad that banks would not lend even to other banks.

I believe strongly in the importance of a strong central bank (the Federal Reserve), as free as possible from political pressures and interference. As a historical note, the Fed and the Treasury have been locked in battle since the Fed was created in 1913, with the Treasury attempting to control the Fed and the Fed fighting fiercely for its independence. I have always been on the Fed side of the argument because I believe monetary policy and crisis management need to be as removed as possible from politics.

For this reason, I am deeply concerned about the degree to which Secretary Paulson appeared to dominate the Federal Reserve during the crisis of 2008 and the degree to which the failure resolution process appeared to be politicized. I believe that the intense political backlash to the bailouts and the TARP legislation is in no small part due to the public perception that the crisis management process was driven by Wall Street for the benefit of Wall Street.

Telephone logs of New York Fed President Geithner subpoenaed by Congress reveal that from September 14, 2008, to November 4, 2008 (election day), Geithner had 185 telephone conversations with Secretary Paulson and 102 conversations with Dan Jester, formerly a close associate of Paulson's at Goldman Sachs, who apparently had an informal very active consulting role at Treasury during the crisis of 2008. During this same period, the phone logs show that Geithner had just 107 conversations with his boss, Fed Chairman Ben Bernanke. In contrast, I recall speaking with Treasury Secretary Regan about bank failures maybe 10 times during my years heading the FDIC during the banking crisis of the 1980s, while I was in continuous contact with Fed Chairman Paul Volcker.

Curiously, the logs show that Mr. Geithner spoke with then Congressman Rahm Emanuel (now chief of staff to President Obama) nine times during this period. Emanuel was not in the leadership of the House—Barney Frank, chairman of the House Financial Services Committee, appears on the log only once. Chris Dodd, chairman of the Senate Banking Committee appears twice, while Speaker of the House Nancy Pelosi does not appear at all. Moreover, according to the phone logs, Geithner spoke 21 times with Larry Summers during this period. Summers, currently President Obama's top economic advisor and Treasury Secretary late in the Clinton Administration, had no position in government during 2008. An obvious question is: What were the calls to Emanuel and Summers about?

Including the conversations with Paulson and Jester, the Geithner phone logs reveal that he had nearly 450 telephone conversations—almost 10 per day—from September 14, 2008, to November 4, 2008, with individuals that I can identify as being affiliated or formerly affiliated with Goldman Sachs. Moreover, the chairman of the New York Fed during this period was a board member and former chief executive officer of Goldman Sachs. Finally, the logs reveal that Geithner had more than 200 additional conversations during this period with the leaders of other major financial institutions. Why were all of these calls necessary? When we made contingency plans to nationalize all of the major banks in the country during the mid-1980s, I do not recall reaching out to any bank executives to ask what they thought of the idea.

In contrast to the hundreds of calls between and among Geithner and the titans of Wall Street, Treasury and political operatives, I can count on my fingers the calls between Geithner and the handful of people who were actively involved in resolving the bank and S&L crises of the 1980s. Another thing that jumps out at me from the logs is the dearth of contact between Geithner and people who could be considered even remotely connected to Main Street.

Regulators use their supervisory and regulatory tools to carry out wide ranging responsibilities over our financial system, including protecting depositors and the economy, maintaining discipline in the markets, limiting moral hazards, minimizing exposure to taxpayers, preserving the deposit insurance fund, keeping credit flowing to worthy borrowers, and maintaining public confidence. Some of these objectives are at odds and choices have to be made.

When push comes to shove, maintaining public confidence should always be priority number one. An extremely important element in maintaining public confidence is to convey that the crisis management and failure resolution processes are fair to the country as a whole, not just a favored few. I believe we flunked that test in 2008 and 2009. I will return to these themes after reviewing the major transactions leading to the panic of 2008.

Bear Stearns

Investment bank Bear Stearns was the first significant casualty of the subprime mortgage mess. The Fed reacted quickly and wisely on March 14, 2008, when it made a $30 billion nonrecourse loan to JPMorgan Chase to be reloaned to Bear Stearns, which was suffering a liquidity crisis. Two days later, the Fed arranged for JPMorgan Chase to purchase Bear Stearns with considerable financial assistance from the Fed.

The rescue of Bear Stearns was a huge statement by the government that it would do everything in its power to restore sanity to the markets. Having rescued Continental Illinois in 1984 in a groundbreaking transaction, I have a special appreciation for what the Fed did.

I had two principal questions at the time, the answers to which were still not evident by early 2010. First, why did the Fed believe it was necessary to force Bear Stearns to sell itself to JPMorgan Chase that weekend rather than simply continuing the liquidity loan as long as necessary? The latter approach would certainly have been less dramatic and more calming. Who knows, perhaps Bear Stearns might have survived the storm or, failing that, the government would have more time to fashion a less expensive resolution.

We intervened at Continental Illinois with a temporary assistance package to calm the markets and give us time to arrange a long-term solution. We made an unprecedented statement that no general creditor would suffer a loss at Continental and that the government was prepared to do whatever it took to address the liquidity crisis. It worked. It calmed the markets with respect to Continental Illinois and the financial system generally, and it gave us months to explore every possible option for dealing with Continental.

Second, why did the Fed believe it appropriate to arrange a quick shotgun marriage between Bear Stearns and JPMorgan Chase? This transaction unnecessarily gave rise to concerns that political games were being played to reward friends or punish enemies, particularly when the Secretary of the Treasury had just two years before been the head of a major Wall Street firm. These concerns would gain more currency as the crisis played out.

IndyMac Bank

The next to fall was IndyMac Bank, a federal savings bank—a thrift institution, not a commercial bank—based in California. It had total assets of $32 billion and was closed July 11, 2008, by the Office of Thrift Supervision.

The FDIC handled the failure as an insured deposit payoff, which means that all depositors above the $100,000 deposit insurance limit then in force and all nondeposit creditors were exposed to loss. It was by far the largest bank failure in U.S. history in which uninsured depositors and other creditors were not made whole. With bank creditors suddenly realizing their investments in banks were much riskier than they thought, tensions rose in the financial markets.

The FDIC estimated that 10,000 of IndyMac customers held about $1 billion of uninsured deposits. The FDIC announced that it would pay uninsured depositors an advance dividend equal to 50 percent of the uninsured amount of their deposits. This was a technique developed by the FDIC in connection with the failure of Penn Square Bank in 1982. It provides uninsured depositors some important liquidity, thereby reducing their hardship, but it still exposes them to significant losses.

When the FDIC protects all depositors, it reduces marketplace discipline and increases the moral hazards. So, in ordinary times, the preferred course is not to protect depositors above the insurance limit. The question is at what point in 2008 should regulators have recognized that we were not in ordinary times? I am not sure policy makers could have foreseen the magnitude of the looming crisis in early July, but I believe it was pretty clear there was much to be concerned about.

To be fair, the FDIC did not have nearly the flexibility in handling bank failures in 2008 that it enjoyed in 1984 when it handled Continental Illinois. The governing law in 1984 required the FDIC to do the "least cost" failure resolution, but it gave the FDIC the ability to use judgment in applying the "cost test." For example, in determining how to handle Continental Illinois, the FDIC could and did consider the impact that an outright failure and insured deposit payoff might have on other banks throughout the country. It was not required to take a myopic view of the failure at hand.

The law was changed by Congress in 1991 because of a misdiagnosis of the causes of the S&L crisis and a political backlash against the too-big-to-fail concept. The FDIC in 2008 was required to do the least-cost solution unless a determination was made that "severe financial conditions" existed. The FDIC had no authority to declare the existence of severe financial conditions unless authorized to do so by the Secretary of the Treasury after consulting with the president and unless the decision was approved by a two-thirds vote of both the FDIC board and the Fed board.

This limitation of the FDIC's authority is hugely unwise. It creates a cumbersome resolutions process, weakens the FDIC, and necessarily politicizes a process that should be run by professionals who are as free as possible from political considerations. We have an independent Fed and FDIC for very good reasons.

To put a finer point on it, the Treasury Department and the White House should not be in charge of bank regulation or failure resolution. They do not have the expertise and they are far too political. Recall that it was Treasury and the Congress that encouraged the Federal Home Loan Bank Board to mask the S&L problems by adopting regulatory accounting rules at odds with generally accepted accounting principles (GAAP). And it was Treasury and the leadership in Congress that promoted the notion that the best solution to the S&L problems was for insolvent institutions with weak management to grow their way out of the problems.

Fannie Mae and Freddie Mac

The markets were concerned for months that Fannie and Freddie, the two mortgage giants called GSEs (government sponsored enterprises), would need government assistance. Senior government officials repeatedly denied the reports and claimed that both institutions had sufficient capital to weather the storm.

Then suddenly, on September 7, not quite two months after the failure of IndyMac, Freddie Mac and Fannie Mae were nationalized. The government takeover was announced by the Treasury Department and the Federal Housing Finance Agency (FHFA), the new regulator of GSEs.

The action placed Fannie Mae and Freddie Mac in conservatorship and put day-to-day management under the control of the FHFA. Treasury Secretary Henry Paulson said that "conservatorship was the only form in which I would commit taxpayer money to the GSEs."

The chief executive officers and the boards of directors of the two organizations were dismissed and dividends were suspended on their common and preferred stock. Common stockholders found their ownership stake in the organizations diluted by 80 percent. Debt holders and mortgages guaranteed by the two organizations were insulated from losses.

Treasury acquired up to $1 billion in senior preferred stock in each organization and said it would stand ready to inject as much as $200 billion in new capital if needed. Treasury also said it would purchase pools of Fannie Mae and Freddie Mac mortgage-backed securities on the open market, beginning with a $5 billion purchase almost immediately.

Two aspects of the takeover of Freddie and Fannie shook financial markets throughout the world. First, there had been the repeated denials by government leaders that Fannie and Freddie might need government help. Leaders dealing with a crisis should never issue a public utterance that has any reasonable chance of being proved false. When Fannie and Freddie were taken over, despite the denials leading up to the event, the public could reasonably conclude that the government leaders who issued the denials were either lying or terribly misinformed. Neither conclusion inspires confidence.

In the early 1980s, when we were facing the massive insolvency of the savings banks and widespread problems in the commercial banks, I received a lot of questions about the adequacy of the FDIC fund. Rather than saying the fund had plenty of money, which I could not guarantee, I said we believed the FDIC fund was sufficient to deal with the problems we could foresee, but if it was not, we would ask Congress for additional funding.

Instead of making a flat-footed statement that Fannie and Freddie had plenty of capital, our leaders would have been well-advised to simply state that Freddie and Fannie were crucial to the economy and the government stood ready to help should the need arise. A statement along those lines might have gone far to stabilize the two mortgage giants and reduce the chances that government intervention would be necessary.

The second aspect of the Fannie and Freddie takeover that rattled the markets was the decision to essentially wipe out the preferred stockholders in each entity. Many foreign governments held preferred stock in these GSEs—among them was China, the largest investor in U.S. government securities. Moreover, foreign governments and other investors had been supplying a fair amount of capital to U.S. banks that had been hit hard by losses generated by mark-to-market accounting. Wiping out preferred stockholders at the two giant GSEs was hardly comforting to investors, whether foreign or domestic. The financial markets were losing confidence in their ability to predict which institutions would fail next and how the U.S. government would handle those failures.

Many domestic banks held large quantities of Fannie and Freddie preferred stock. According to a survey conducted by the American Bankers Association in mid-September 2008, more than one-fourth of the nation's banks lost a combined $10 billion to $15 billion in the wake of the federal government's takeover of Fannie Mae and Freddie Mac. The ABA estimated that the impact on bank capital would reduce bank lending capacity by more than $100 billion at a time when the government was pushing for increased lending to bolster the economy.

Until the government takeover of Fannie and Freddie, their preferred stock was considered to have almost as little risk as U.S. government securities and was so recognized by the 20 percent risk weighting the stock was given under risk-based capital standards developed by the bank regulatory agencies. Wiping out Fannie and Freddie preferred stock was a boneheaded idea. It sent shock waves throughout the world and added fuel to the conflagration in the financial system.

I wonder to this day why the government did not just issue a temporary guarantee of Fannie and Freddie's liabilities in order to restore confidence in them during the crisis. The Treasury issued a guarantee of money market funds on September 28 after the failure of Lehman Brothers panicked financial markets throughout the world. Why did the crisis management leaders at Treasury and elsewhere think it wise to nationalize these two GSEs and create considerable instability in the world's financial markets instead of doing something less dramatic and more calming?

A few lawmakers in Congress, notably former Rep. Richard Baker (R-La.), had been arguing for years that the activities of Fannie and Freddie posed excessive risk to the economy and exposed taxpayers to a potentially huge liability because the two government sponsored enterprises were out of control. But Baker and his allies were unable to persuade Congress to enact legislation that would rein in Fannie and Freddie, and by the fall of 2008, their worst concerns became a reality.

Freddie and Fannie played a very major role in creating the financial mess in which we found ourselves in 2008 and the Clinton Administration and Congress played very substantial roles in promoting uncontrolled, high-risk growth at Fannie and Freddie during the 1990s by urging them to lower their credit standards and provide more housing loans to less credit worthy borrowers. There was a very close and symbiotic relationship between Freddie and Fannie and the government. The leaders of these two giant quasi-public agencies were given enormous compensation packages for doing the public's business. They developed tremendous lobbying machines to help them gain new powers and keep reformers like then Congressman Richard Baker at bay.

The next time you hear some member of Congress railing against the corporate greed that created the crisis of 2008, keep in mind that Congress and the Clinton Administration kept feeding the beast and refused to rein in its excesses. Ask that lawmaker whether he or she ever voted to curtail Fannie's or Freddie's explosive, high-risk growth strategies.

Lehman Brothers

Another bombshell hit the financial markets five days after Freddie and Fannie were nationalized, when Lehman Brothers, a large investment banking firm, was allowed to fail. Lehman Brothers had troubles with its commercial real estate portfolio, among other things. When the losses started to mount in mid-2008, Lehman came under pressure from Treasury Secretary Paulson to find a merger partner or new capital, but Lehman could do neither. Because of JPMorgan Chase's rescue of Bear Stearns in March and the federal government's takeover of Fannie Mae and Freddie Mac in early September, it was widely anticipated in the financial markets that Lehman was destined for a government bailout as well.

Shockingly, and almost inexplicably, that did not happen. On September 12, Lehman got the word that, unlike Bear Stearns, it would get no government assistance to avert bankruptcy. One potential last-minute acquirer of Lehman was Bank of America, but BofA opted instead to pursue the acquisition of Merrill Lynch, another troubled investment bank. Barclays Bank was the last-chance suitor for Lehman, but the deal was complicated by the need for approval from the British government, which could not be accomplished quickly enough. So Lehman declared bankruptcy on Sunday, September 14, before the markets opened in Europe and Asia.

The global financial markets were stunned by the government's decision to let Lehman go bankrupt. The message heard was that the U.S. government would no longer bail out failing companies because it creates moral hazards and encourages firms to engage in risky behavior.

Months later, we were told that the government had no choice in the matter because no buyers could be found for Lehman. I take that bit of revisionist history with a very large dose of salt. In my experience, there are buyers for virtually anything, depending on the terms offered. And even if absolutely no buyers could be found at anything approaching a reasonable price, the government could have funded Lehman, as it did Bear Stearns before arranging the sale to JPMorgan Chase, or it could have recapitalized Lehman just as it did with another failing giant less than a week later.

The FDIC had no buyers for Continental Illinois in 1984 on terms we considered reasonable. That did not lead us to conclude that the smart thing to do was let Continental Illinois file for bankruptcy and cause panic throughout the world. Instead, we structured an unprecedented transaction to keep Continental Illinois afloat and give us time to work out a longer-term solution.

Months after the Lehman debacle, Paulson claimed the big problem was that the Federal Reserve lacked statutory authority to make a loan to an investment bank that did not possess the appropriate collateral. He indicated that the size of the loan necessary to salvage Lehman's balance sheet was in the billions of dollars and the besieged investment bank did not have enough collateral to pull that off. Yet four days later, the government found a way to prevent a much larger and more complex company, American International Group (AIG), from going into bankruptcy. The collateral for the Fed loan to AIG was the company itself. It is far from clear why that same approach could not have been used at Lehman.

It was a colossal mistake to allow Lehman to go into bankruptcy in the middle of a worldwide financial crisis. I was not in the room so I cannot say with certainty why it was allowed to fail. While I am not a betting man, I would be willing to wager a lot of money that it was because government leaders were too concerned about being criticized for bailing out yet another firm, and they significantly underestimated the impact Lehman's failure would have on the markets.

In any event, our leaders clearly had insufficient appreciation for the idea that priority number one in a financial crisis must be to maintain public confidence. The Lehman failure reinforced the perception that there was no coherent and consistent plan in place to keep things from spinning out of control and that Washington was too focused on making the right political decisions.

American International Group (AIG)

Nine days after the Fannie-Freddie takeover and four days after Lehman's demise was disclosed, AIG, one of the world's largest insurance companies, was the next major casualty.

One of AIG's affiliates (AIG Financial Products, based in London) crippled the insurance giant. It suffered mark-to-market losses in connection with credit default swaps on mortgage-related securities and investors feared that more losses were in store.

AIG's credit rating was downgraded and private equity firms and banks were afraid to come to the rescue for fear of a government takeover that would wipe them out.

The government in effect nationalized AIG on September 16. The Federal Reserve agreed to lend AIG $85 billion on exceedingly harsh terms, including the government gaining a 79.9 percent equity interest in AIG.

The Fed announced that the loan would be made by the Federal Reserve Bank of New York, adding that the secured loan was designed to protect the interests of the U.S. government and taxpayers:

> The Board determined that, in current circumstances, a disorderly failure of AIG could add to already significant levels of financial market fragility and lead to substantially higher borrowing costs, reduced household wealth, and materially weaker economic performance.

Among other things, the Fed disclosed that AIG was one of the 10 most popular stocks held in 401(k) retirement plans and that AIG's collapse might cause a catastrophic run on mutual funds. It is not clear to me how confiscating 80 percent of the stock of AIG in exchange for an $85 billion liquidity loan enhanced the position of the retirement plans and mutual funds that owned AIG's stock.

Testifying before the Senate Banking Committee on September 24, Fed Chairman Ben Bernanke added:

> The Federal Reserve took this action because it judged that, in light of the prevailing market conditions and the size and composition of AIG's obligations, a disorderly failure of AIG would have severely threatened global financial stability and, consequently, the performance of the U.S. economy. To mitigate concerns that this action would exacerbate moral hazard and encourage inappropriate risk-taking in the future, the Federal Reserve ensured

that the terms of the credit extended to AIG imposed significant costs and constraints on the firm's owners, managers, and creditors. The chief executive officer has been replaced. The collateral for the loan is the company itself, together with its subsidiaries.

AIG essentially got caught in an ever-increasing liquidity squeeze that jeopardized its very existence. The government stepped in to stave off a potential collapse of the global financial system. That action may have helped prevent the collapse of the global financial system, but there were adverse consequences nonetheless.

The government rescue wiped out AIG stockholders, which had a chilling effect on the markets. If AIG, at one time the largest financial institution in the world based on the value of its stock, was being swept under by the global tidal wave, was any financial institution safe?

I agreed with the decision to help AIG. I had serious reservations about the harshness of the terms imposed on AIG, which essentially destroyed one of our country's most prized financial institutions. It would not surprise me if taxpayers take a big loss on the loans to AIG, considering the damage that was done to the company by its nationalization. I am not trying to deflect blame from the management decisions at AIG that created the problems. I am saying that the government's cure likely made matters much worse.

My take at the time was that AIG was suffering from a liquidity squeeze rather than insolvency and that the company had enormous value if it could make it through the crisis. Ordinarily in a situation like this, the company's bank lenders would step in, provide liquidity, and require changes in management and the business plan. They would be rewarded handsomely for any additional credit they advanced plus they would avoid big losses on loans they already had outstanding with the company.

When we rescued Continental Illinois, Paul Volcker and I convened an emergency meeting of the largest bank creditors of

Continental. We told them the FDIC and the Fed were willing to intervene to arrest the liquidity crisis at Continental before it infected the entire financial system, but we needed help from the banks to present a united front to the world. We asked the banks to participate in the FDIC capital infusion and to increase their lines of credit to Continental. After 24 hours of sometimes intense wrangling, we were able to announce to the world that the Fed, the FDIC, and the nation's largest banks had come together to stabilize Continental Illinois. Why was this not done at AIG?

I do not know why the existing bank creditors could not be persuaded to join in a rescue plan for AIG, particularly if the government agreed to limit their risks. I have not heard that they were even asked. Nor do I know why the existing bank creditors of AIG were bailed out and were not required to give something in return.

Former Treasury Secretary Paulson and current Treasury Secretary Geithner explained at hearings by the House Committee on Oversight and Government Reform in early 2010 that there was too little time to get a deal done with the banks and the government had too little leverage. As someone who, along with Paul Volcker, got the seven largest banks on board with the rescue of Continental Illinois within a 24-hour period, I find this explanation less than compelling. Moreover, at a recent hearing of the Financial Crisis Inquiry Commission, the chief executive of Goldman Sachs, Lloyd Blankfein, indicated that to his knowledge, his firm was not asked to make concessions.

It concerns me that one of the large bank creditors of AIG was Goldman Sachs, the firm that Paulson headed before becoming Treasury Secretary, and that Paulson reportedly had meetings with the head of Goldman to discuss the bailout of AIG. I am not charging that either of them was improperly motivated, but the appearance of a conflict of interest is difficult not to acknowledge.

My former employer, First Kentucky, was a major creditor of the Butchers when I left for the FDIC. I did not have a single conversation while at the FDIC with anyone at First Kentucky about the Butcher banks prior to their failure. To this day, I do not know if First Kentucky suffered a loss at the Butcher banks.

Washington Mutual (WaMu)

Eighteen days after the Fannie and Freddie takeovers and nine days after the AIG nationalization, another giant institution toppled. Washington Mutual Bank—or WaMu as it was nick-named—was the nation's largest S&L, not a commercial bank. WaMu had assets of $307 billion. As such, WaMu's demise goes down as the largest FDIC-insured bank failure of all time in terms of assets and roughly tied with Continental Illinois in terms of relative size in the financial system.

On September 25, the FDIC announced that it facilitated a transaction in which JPMorgan Chase acquired the banking operations of WaMu. In the announcement, the FDIC said that "all depositors are fully protected, and there will be no cost to the Deposit Insurance Fund."

"For all depositors and other customers of Washington Mutual Bank, this is simply a combination of two banks," said FDIC Chairman Sheila C. Bair. "For bank customers, it will be a seamless transition. There will be no interruption in services and bank customers should expect business as usual. . . ."

This, too, was a destabilizing transaction. Although the FDIC chose to cover all uninsured deposits, $20 billion in WaMu bonds were left uncovered and those bondholders suffered a total loss. Just as significant for the markets was the fact that one of WaMu's largest investors—the private equity firm Texas Pacific Group (TPG)—was wiped out.

TPG had no hand in creating the problems at WaMu. It came to the rescue of the troubled bank a few months before the failure with $7 billion of fresh capital in the form of convertible preferred stock—no good deed goes unpunished.

Until the resolution of WaMu, banks generally had reasonable access to the capital markets to raise fresh equity. Citigroup, Wachovia, National City, and WaMu itself were notable examples. Once the bondholders and TPG were wiped out at WaMu, the ballgame for new private sector capital was over. Who wants to invest in a troubled financial institution if the federal government is going to leave you high and dry in the event the institution cannot be saved?

Even at this late stage of the crisis, government policy makers were still focused heavily on not bailing out creditors. That was about to change as the financial system throughout the world was freezing up. Banks were refusing to lend money even to other banks, as no one could be sure which institution would fail next or how the government would handle the failure.

It was in the middle of these cascading disasters that Secretary Paulson and Fed chairman Bernanke rushed to Capitol Hill to make their urgent plea for $700 billion in taxpayer money to bail out the financial system.

Chapter 14

The $700 Billion Bailout

T he government was scrambling madly to head off a complete collapse of the global financial system in the fall of 2008. In quick succession two huge thrifts failed, mortgage giants Fannie Mae and Freddie Mac were nationalized, investment bank Bear Stearns was saved with massive government assistance, Lehman Brothers was condemned to bankruptcy, and insurance giant AIG was nationalized. Rumors were flying about other major financial institutions.

Against this backdrop, Treasury Secretary Henry Paulson and Fed Chairman Ben Bernanke testified before Congress on September 23, pleading for $700 billion in taxpayer funds to purchase toxic assets from financial institutions (the Troubled Asset Relief Program, or TARP). They argued it was needed to save the financial system and the U.S. economy from utter chaos or financial Armageddon.

They said the need was so urgent that Congress should act without hearings, debates, or significant amendments. The unthinkable occurred when Congress authorized a $700 billion outlay of taxpayer money within 13 days of the initial testimony by Paulson and Bernanke.

■■■

I was appalled by the Paulson plan and urged Congress to take a cautious, considered approach before signing off on the largest bailout program in the history of the world. At a minimum, I felt Congress should examine why the program was needed, whether the program was likely to work as intended, whether there were alternatives, and what safeguards were needed to control potential abuses. Taxpayers deserved nothing less.

I believed then, and continue to believe, that the plan to purchase $700 billion of toxic assets would have been a colossal waste of taxpayer money. I viewed it as a plan concocted by Wall Street for the exclusive benefit of Wall Street. Banks would not sell the assets to the government unless offered more than the assets were worth. Investors would not purchase the assets unless the government agreed to take less than they were worth. If investors and banks were in agreement about the value of the assets, the government program would not have been necessary. So by definition the program was destined to have taxpayers subsidize banks by overpaying for toxic assets and enrich investors by selling the assets for less than they were worth.

Another obvious flaw in the plan was that taking $700 billion of bad assets off the books of a $14 trillion financial system was a drop in the bucket and would stimulate bank lending by at most $700 billion, which would not have a meaningful impact on the economy. I argued that the FDIC had existing authority to purchase capital in banks if the Treasury declared a financial emergency. Since banks generally can lend 8 to 10 times their capital, $700 billion of capital infusions (not that such a large amount was needed) would have increased bank lending capacity by some $6 trillion. No new legislation was needed to authorize capital infusions by the FDIC.

The Administration and the leaders of Congress were hell-bent on forging ahead. At the outset, taxpayers—and Congress for that matter—were told little more than the simple refrain that "chaos will ensue if we don't authorize the $700 billion."

When resistance started growing, a new justification began circulating: that the money market mutual funds were under a great deal of pressure, with investors losing confidence in them and asking for their money back. But that concern should have been allayed by the Treasury's September 19 announcement of a 100 percent U.S. guarantee of the money market funds.

Of course, the money market fund guarantee was Exhibit A in the case for not rushing into solutions without assessing unintended consequences. No one paused long enough to consider that if every penny in money market funds was backed 100 percent by the government, banks and S&Ls with their meager $100,000 FDIC insurance limit would not be able to maintain their funding.

Why keep money in an FDIC-insured bank when you can put unlimited amounts in 100 percent government-guaranteed money market funds that pay higher interest rates? If deposits fled the banks in favor of money market funds, who would make new loans to support economic growth? Banks cannot make loans without deposits.

When this issue was brought to Treasury's attention by the American Bankers Association a day or two after the money market fund guarantee was issued, Treasury moved quickly to alleviate the problem by providing that the guarantee was limited to money already on hand in the funds, not to new money. If the principal bailout proponents overlooked something as obvious as this, it hardly inspired confidence in the team that was in charge of crisis management.

The other rationale for immediate congressional action on the $700 billion bailout was that bank depositors were starting to get panicky. I doubted that because panicky depositors usually lose faith in specific institutions, not the financial system at large.

If depositor confidence were at the root of all this, why should we enact an emergency program to purchase $700 billion of bad real estate loans to solve the problem? The full faith and credit of the U.S. government already stood behind the FDIC. If we needed to be more aggressive, the FDIC could have declared that until the crisis ended, all bank deposits and other senior debt of banks and thrifts would be protected in bank failures.

New legislation was not needed for the FDIC to issue a broad guarantee of depositors. It could be done under existing law with approval of the Treasury and the Fed. It would have been a virtually costless approach, as there is no doubt in my mind that in the climate of a worldwide financial crisis, no bank of consequence was going to be allowed to fail in a way that caused depositors or other general creditors to take losses. Since we were already there in reality, we might as well let the public know it.

In any event, the cost of the temporary guarantee of all depositors would have been a small fraction of the $700 billion toxic asset purchase. An additional benefit of this approach would have been to put community banks on the same footing as the largest banks because depositors above the insurance limit are less convinced, for good reason, that the government will bail them out of a small bank than out of a mega bank. If one thing has been clear throughout 2008, 2009, and early 2010, the best interests of community banks have not been a priority of government leaders.

The FDIC did take action by adopting the Temporary Liquidity Guarantee Program not long after the bailout bill became law to reassure depositors and other creditors of banks. The plan was convoluted and difficult for most depositors and other creditors to comprehend. Moreover, the FDIC charged banks premiums for the new guarantees it issued, draining capital from the banks. While I preferred a simpler program, it helped to stabilize the banking system far more than the TARP.

■■■

If there were other reasons for taxpayers to fork over $700 billion, they needed to be disclosed and debated in Congress. We needed to know before rushing to judgment whether the $700 billion purchase of toxic assets would in fact work. I argued strenuously that it would not, and the Treasury ultimately agreed because none of the $700 billion authorized by Congress was used to purchase toxic assets.

Within two weeks after passage of the TARP bill, Paulson announced that the money would be used to purchase capital instead of toxic assets. Treasury promptly began investing the TARP money in Wall Street firms, insurance companies, and finance companies. To add insult to injury, Paulson used the TARP money, which was clearly intended to be used for financial institutions, to bail out Chrysler and General Motors and their finance arms, Chrysler Financial and GMAC. He took this action after Congress specifically debated and rejected a bailout plan for the two auto companies! I was incensed, as were tens of millions of taxpayers throughout the land.

In any event, Congress completed action October 3 and President George W. Bush quickly signed the TARP legislation. The main provision of the new law provided up to $700 billion to the Treasury to buy mortgages and other assets clogging the balance sheets of financial institutions. In addition, the new law:

- Temporarily increased the insurance ceiling on federally guaranteed deposits from $100,000 to $250,000
- Authorized the Securities and Exchange Commission to suspend mark-to-market accounting, so-called fair value accounting, under Financial Accounting Standards No. 157

- Allowed the Federal Reserve to pay interest on bank reserves
- Temporarily increased the borrowing limits at the U.S. Treasury for the FDIC and the credit union insurance fund
- Extended the existing law providing tax forgiveness on the cancellation of mortgage debt

On October 14, the government announced that it was abandoning the toxic asset purchase plan and was instead taking several coordinated actions, including the investment of federal funds in U.S. banks, "to protect the U.S. economy, to strengthen public confidence in our financial institutions, and to foster the robust functioning of our credit markets."

One of the steps was a voluntary Capital Purchase Program (CPP) under which a broad array of financial institutions were eligible to participate by selling preferred shares to the U.S. government on attractive terms that protect the taxpayer. Under the CPP, the U.S. Treasury was to make available $250 billion capital to U.S. financial institutions.

It is quite telling that several of the nine large institutions taking the initial $125 billion insisted in their joint meeting with Treasury that they did not want the capital injection. They were told in no uncertain terms that the program was not voluntary for any of the nine institutions—all were required to accept the government's (that is, taxpayers') capital contribution. Treasury wanted to disguise the one or two banks that really needed the money by also giving the money to banks that did not need it. I guess that is what one does when playing with other people's money with no meaningful restraints on how to use it.

■■■

Let us review the bidding and think about this for a moment. Congress and the American people were told that $700 billion in emergency funding was urgently needed to purchase toxic assets from financial institutions if we were to avoid financial

153

Armageddon. This was justified on the basis of a potential run on money market funds that Treasury had already halted by issuing a poorly conceived 100 percent guarantee of their liabilities.

Further justification was that depositors might begin to panic and create a run on banks, something that did not happen when 3,000 banks and thrifts failed during the 1980s. But the FDIC already had authority to guarantee bank creditors against loss and in fact used that preexisting authority shortly after Congress enacted the bailout legislation.

Immediately after the legislation was enacted, Treasury decided that the plan to purchase toxic assets was not feasible and instead invested in the capital of banks, something the FDIC had authority to do without the legislation. To make matters worse, several of the initial nine recipients of the capital were ordered to take it against their wishes. Hundreds of other banks took the money because they thought it was a good deal or because their regulators pressured them to accept the capital "just in case." On top of all that, Secretary Paulson used the TARP money to bail out two auto companies after Congress considered and refused to pass direct legislation to do so.

I am still trying to figure out where financial Armageddon fits in this picture!

A second step under the October 14 announcement was to exercise a systemic risk exception to the Federal Deposit Insurance Act enabling the FDIC to temporarily guarantee the senior debt of all FDIC-insured institutions and their holding companies, as well as deposits in checking accounts. Paulson made the systemic risk determination after receiving a recommendation from the FDIC and the Fed and after consulting with the president.

The third step mentioned in the October 14 announcement was the previously disclosed program for the Fed to purchase commercial paper. This program was designed to further increase access to funding for businesses in all sectors of the economy. The government said the Fed's Commercial Paper Funding Facility program would provide a broad backstop for the commercial paper market.

The Fed used a great deal of ingenuity in devising a host of measures to provide liquidity to a beleaguered financial system over the ensuing months—measures that continued in effect into 2010. The Fed tried one program and if it did not work, other programs were implemented until the right mix was found. The Fed measures, combined with the guarantees issued by the FDIC, did a great deal to calm the financial markets. They could have been done without the TARP legislation.

A more deliberate legislative process on the bailout legislation might have given Congress the chance to consider a program it enacted in the banking and thrift crisis of the 1980s. This was a "net worth certificate" program, which the FDIC implemented successfully for the deeply troubled savings bank industry.

The net worth certificate program was designed to shore up the capital of weak banks to give them more time to resolve their problems. The program involved no subsidy and no cash outlay. Banks entering the program had to agree to strict oversight from the FDIC, including oversight of compensation of top executives and removal of poor management.

If the FDIC had resurrected the net worth certificate program in the 2008 crisis, the capital position of banks would have been bolstered enough to give them a shot at rehabilitation. No taxpayer money would have been spent, and the FDIC would likely have saved considerable money.

Interestingly, the FDIC used the net worth certificate program in 29 banks in the 1980s. Only seven of the banks failed while 22 survived. The seven banks that failed cost the FDIC $480 million, or 0.8 percent of their assets, compared to average losses of 15 percent of assets on failed banks not covered by the net worth certificate program (the FDIC's losses on failed banks in 2009 were running above 20 percent).

In particular, I thought resurrecting the net worth certificates would have been a great program for struggling community banks that qualified for the program. Virtually all of the government's efforts in 2008, 2009, and early 2010 were focused on protecting the largest financial firms in the country while community banks continued to drop like flies.

■ ■ ■

I opposed the bailout legislation because I felt it would be a waste of taxpayer money to purchase $700 billion of toxic assets from the banks. I believed there were much better ways to accomplish what needed to be done, and I offered an alternative four-point plan in an op-ed in the *Washington Post* on September 27, when the bailout legislation was under consideration by Congress.

I believed then and continue to believe that this four-point program would have done everything the TARP legislation could do, would have cost taxpayers little if any money, would have been more reassuring to the public, would not have politicized the crisis the way the Paulson plan did, and would not have undermined public confidence in our government and financial system the way the TARP legislation did.

My suggested plan called for:

1. The SEC to immediately reimpose on short sellers the Depression-era regulations on speculative abuses the SEC removed in 2007
2. The FDIC to find that severe financial conditions existed and declare that all creditors and other depositors of banks would be protected in bank failures during the period of the emergency
3. The SEC to move immediately to suspend the mark-to-market accounting rules adopted by the SEC and the FASB in the preceding decade
4. The FDIC to use its emergency powers to enhance capital in banks

In the end, some version of each of the four recommendations I offered was implemented after the TARP bill was enacted— indeed, except for the mark-to-market accounting reforms, almost *immediately* after TARP was enacted. And the plan to purchase toxic assets I so adamantly opposed as a waste of taxpayer money was jettisoned before it got started.

■■■

In retrospect, was the TARP legislation good or bad for the country? The powers that be—those who recommended and those who voted for TARP—say it helped to stabilize the financial system.

I believe that any objective analysis would conclude that the TARP legislation did nothing to stabilize the financial system that could not have been done without it. Moreover, the negative aspects of the TARP legislation far outweighed any possible benefit.

The things that helped stabilize the financial system were:

- The enhanced guarantees of deposits and other bank and bank holding company debt by the FDIC
- The FDIC handling both Wachovia and Citibank in late 2008 in a way that did not expose creditors of those organizations to losses and continuing that policy with respect to large troubled banks into 2009 and beyond
- The various programs implemented by the Fed to provide liquidity to the financial markets
- The SEC's reimposition of regulations on short sellers
- The SEC and FASB backing off to a limited extent on mark-to-market accounting

What about the capital infusions under TARP? First, to the extent needed, they could have and should have been handled by the FDIC under existing law. Second, the point of the capital infusion program in my mind was to replace capital destroyed by mark-to-market accounting so that lost lending capacity could be replaced. That potential benefit was nullified when the government retroactively placed punitive conditions on the capital infusions (that is, no dividends and severe restrictions on executive pay). For the capital to be used to support increased lending, it needed to be considered at least semipermanent capital, but the restrictions accompanying the capital forced the banks to repay it as quickly as possible. It could not be relied on to support new lending. Third, the capital program administered by the Treasury was terribly disruptive to the financial system, as very serious mistakes were made in administering the program.

The first major mistake was when Secretary Paulson called the CEOs of nine of the largest financial companies into his office with great fanfare and ordered them to take TARP money, which several of the banks clearly did not need or want. Hundreds of smaller banks were pressured by their regulators to take the money, "just in case." The entire industry was stigmatized and severely wounded politically—wounds from which it will likely take years if not decades to recover.

The damage was compounded when President Obama's new Treasury secretary, Timothy Geithner, announced publicly on February 10, 2009, that the 19 largest TARP recipients would be required to undergo a "stress test" to determine their ability to survive under various economic scenarios. Stress tests have been performed by banks and bank regulators routinely for as long as I can remember. The decision to announce publicly that the 19 financial institutions would undergo special stress tests was amateurish—the CEO of one large bank publicly called it "asinine." Senior bank regulators were appalled.

What good could come of it? Things were just beginning to stabilize in the banking industry and now new seeds of doubt were being sown. Which firms would flunk the test, and what would be the consequence? If the government did not reveal the results, the public would fear the worst. If the government announced the results and said everyone passed, many would not believe it. If the government announced the names of the firms that flunked the test, it would likely set off bank runs.

The reaction in the markets was swift and negative. The Dow Jones Industrial Average stood at 8200 prior to the announcement and declined to just over 6500 over the next month. The KBW Bank Stock Index dropped from 31 to below 19 during the same period.

The government, forced to do damage control, announced that none of the 19 large banks would be permitted to fail creating 19 new too big to fail banks. Imagine how that announcement was received by the firms smaller than the 19 stress test banks that had to compete with them for funding!

The results of the stress tests were finally made public on May 7 with Chairman Bernanke declaring that all 19 banks had sufficient total capital to absorb higher losses under a worst case scenario, but that "roughly half" needed to place more emphasis on common equity. The announcement was anticlimactic and demonstrated that the exercise was pointless and needlessly destructive.

Another major mistake was that the capital infusion program was heavily focused on stabilizing the largest banks and did precious little to support the community banks that do so much to help small businesses and consumers throughout our nation's smaller cities and towns. Countless smaller banks were turned away because they could not demonstrate they would be viable *without the TARP money*. I had recommended that the test should be whether the bank would likely be viable *with the TARP money*. The Treasury clearly applied a different standard to the community banks than it did to some of the largest banks—19 of which it declared too big to fail. The rest of the banks were apparently deemed too small to save.

We have put independent agencies such as the FDIC and the Fed in charge of regulating banks and handling bank failures and crises for good reason. They are staffed with experienced professionals and are insulated from politics to the best of our ability to do so.

Treasury is not experienced in bank regulation or in bank crisis management. Recall that Treasury thought it was a grand idea to mask the S&L problems and let insolvent S&Ls grow out of their problems. A major flaw in the TARP program is that it handed Treasury a blank check for $700 billion and gave it broad authority to regulate the banking system, which it is ill equipped to do.

■■■

Enormous damage was done to the economy and in turn to the financial system by the highly inflammatory rhetoric used by government leaders—from the president and the Treasury secretary to congressional leaders from both parties—to sell the TARP program to a doubting Congress and public. They got their legislation but scared the wits out of the public in the process. Wallets slammed shut and the economy flatlined in October.

Proponents of the TARP legislation warned that the Dow would drop by at least 1,000 points if the bill were not passed. Once the bill passed, the markets sobered up to the reality that Congress just authorized $850 billion (including $150 billion of pork added to the TARP bill to buy votes for passage) the Treasury did not have to pay for a bill that would do no good. The Dow sank like a rock from 10,831 on October 1, 2008, to 8175 on October 27. It continued its downward spiral to a low of 6547 on March 9, 2009. It is difficult to imagine how rejection of the bill could have produced worse results.

Chapter 15

Never Again

The panic of 2008 absolutely should not have happened. Its seeds were sown by our failure to understand the lessons of the 1980s and our misguided responses to that crisis. The Senseless Panic of 2008 led to a collapse of the economy and caused enormous pain to millions of people. It must never happen again.

I cannot emphasize enough how important it is that we understand the causes of the financial crisis in 2008 and that we enact the right reforms this time. Those who do not remember *and understand* history will repeat it.

The S&L crisis was caused by the failure of our political leaders to keep inflation in check during the 1970s, which led to interest rates of a magnitude never before witnessed in this country—interest rates so high that almost no financial institution or borrower could withstand the onslaught. The problems were compounded by the failure of political and industry leaders

161

to reform the S&L charter and bring it into the modern era a decade before the crisis.

A very bad situation turned into a disaster when the Reagan Administration and congressional leaders refused to tackle the problems and instead decided to let S&Ls with poor management and little or no capital grow their way out of their problems. In the five-year period from 1984, when I warned Treasury Secretary Jim Baker of the looming S&L crisis, to 1989, when the first Bush Administration and Congress moved to clean up the S&L mess, the cost of resolution increased nearly 10-fold from an estimated $15 billion to nearly $150 billion (or roughly $450 billion in terms relative to today's federal budget).

These losses did not need to occur. The FDIC faced up to very similar problems in the savings bank industry, allowing savings banks to get through the very difficult economic times but not allowing them to increase their risk profile. The result was roughly $2 billion of losses to the FDIC and none to taxpayers.

We reacted to the S&L crisis by blaming "greedy" bankers, just as many have done with the crisis of 2008. It is a politically easy target that deflects attention away from the real issues. Someone once said that blaming greed for bank failures is akin to blaming gravity for airplane crashes. Greed, like gravity, is a force of nature. Greed is an important force in our free enterprise system. The government should recognize that greed exists and control it, just as the government recognizes that airplanes will fall from the skies if planes are not properly maintained and operated by skilled professionals.

We reacted to the S&L crisis by declaring that market forces would be more effective in regulating and controlling risks in the financial system than regulators. Compounding the problem of overreliance on market forces to regulate the financial system, our disillusionment with the S&L regulators also moved us to an increased reliance on models and rules rather than judgment and experience.

Market forces and models are useful tools but strong supervision and regulation should always be the first line of defense in protecting our financial system. Particularly in a crisis, we need to rely heavily on the judgment of trained professionals who are insulated as much as possible from political pressures.

Overreliance on markets and models led the SEC and its sidekick FASB to put into place the highly procyclical and ultimately very destructive mark-to-market accounting system, despite strong warnings from the secretary of the Treasury, the chairman of the Fed and the chairman of the FDIC that it would create greater volatility in banking and lead to severe credit crunches.

Reliance on market forces and models led the SEC to challenge the judgmental approach to establishing loan loss reserves and to the creation of procyclical models that understate reserves in good times and overstate them in bad times. The same flawed thinking led bank regulators to create the backward-looking Basel models for setting capital levels in banks. Capital needs are understated in boom years and overstated in difficult times, making it more difficult to restore lending and turn around the economy.

The SEC added fuel by allowing Wall Street firms to greatly increase their leverage in 2005 at the height of the boom. Two years later, just when the bubble was about to burst, the SEC removed the Depression-era protections against abuses by short sellers of securities.

Congress established a highly procyclical method for assessing FDIC premiums. In good times, when the FDIC fund was flush, banks were not required to pay premiums. In times of trouble, banks were hit with very large special assessments, which made it more difficult for them to lend.

Congress enacted statutory Prompt Corrective Action rules that discriminate against smaller banks and make it difficult for regulators to use judgment during times of severe financial distress.

Finally, Congress neutered the FDIC's crisis management abilities by requiring approval from the White House, Treasury, and the Fed before the FDIC can use its emergency powers in times of severe stress.

Businesses, consumers, and the financial system became over-leveraged during the decade from 1995 to 2005. Allowing loan securitizations, derivatives, and swaps to be taken off bank balance sheets was an important element in this, as were the pro-cyclical rules on capital and loan loss reserves. Many economists believe monetary policy also played a major role. And there is no question that the uncontrolled growth of Fannie Mae and Freddie Mac and their movement to riskier mortgage products propelled the housing bubble.

The boom had to come to an end. The markets and policy makers were hoping for a soft landing and for a time it seemed we were going to achieve one. But then the combined effects of the procyclical accounting and regulatory rules took over and turned the hoped-for soft landing into a very turbulent ride. At that point, ineffective crisis management nearly destroyed the financial system and the economy.

Late in 2009, the Obama Administration and the Congress were debating proposals on how to fix the system. Unfortunately, they were moving much faster than warranted, were debating unimportant ancillary issues and were not addressing the issues that really must be addressed.

Because it is such a moving target, there is little point in going into detail on the Administration's original proposal, which formed the basis for the bill in the House, but I will give a few examples of how far wide of the mark it is:

- It would eliminate industrial loan companies, which had nothing to do with the crisis, but does not deal with Fannie Mae and Freddie Mac, which were at the heart of the crisis and remain wards of the state.

- It proposes an exceedingly minor reorganization of the regulatory structure that failed us in this crisis instead of a clearly warranted sweeping regulatory overhaul.
- It purports to address the problem of too-big-to-fail firms but instead permanently extends the federal safety net and the exposure of taxpayers beyond banking to all companies with financial activities and delegates the authority to accomplish this to regulators so as not to put Congress in the uncomfortable position of actually having to vote to spend our money on future bailouts.
- It proposes a badly needed Systemic Risk Council to monitor developing systemic risks and deal with them before they get out of hand, but instead of making it an independent agency turns it into a handmaiden of the Treasury and the other financial agencies it should be overseeing.
- It does not even mention the procyclical accounting and regulatory rules that played a leading role in creating the panic of 2008.
- It proposes a new bureaucracy in the form of the Consumer Financial Protection Agency to take over the consumer protection functions of the federal banking agencies, which will almost certainly weaken consumer protection for customers of banks and make it more difficult and expensive for consumers and small businesses to obtain loans. There are ways to enhance consumer protections without limiting the ability of banking regulators to use their considerable resources and powers over banks to directly enforce consumer compliance in banks.

One can only hope the bill will undergo significant improvement as it wends its way through Congress. It is distressing that the Administration does not seem to understand what the problems are in our financial system, much less their solutions.

The measures we should implement to help prevent it from happening again are straightforward.

Systemic Risk Council

No one was tending the store during the past two decades when a host of counterproductive reforms were put in place and when the financial system, businesses, and consumers were becoming overleveraged. We desperately need a strong and independent Systemic Risk Council (SRC) to monitor the financial system and the economy generally to detect and blow the whistle on growing systemic risks.

The SRC should be headed by a presidential appointee, confirmed by the Senate, and should have its own staff, probably numbering in the hundreds. It should have an advisory board consisting of the secretary of the Treasury and the heads of the major financial agencies. The SRC should not be a regulator but should be a watchdog on Treasury and the regulators. It should have access to every piece of information relating to the financial system.

The Obama Administration proposed a systemic risk regulator dominated by Treasury and the other financial regulators. A systemic risk regulator controlled by the agencies it should be overseeing would do more harm than good by diffusing responsibility and providing a false sense of security.

The other critical flaw in the Administration's plan for a systemic risk regulator is that it would become a super-regulator dominated by Treasury that could engage in bailouts of large nonbank financial firms and spend taxpayer money in much the same way Treasury did under the TARP legislation. It would spread the federal safety net and greatly increase moral hazards. I hope all taxpayers have had their fill of that. I know I have.

Too Big to Fail

The Administration, Congressional leaders and others are making a lot of noise about "too big to fail" financial institutions, blaming the crisis of 2008 on them and proclaiming that we should abolish the too-big-to-fail doctrine once and for all.

The first thing to note is that, despite the rhetoric, no proposal to date would in fact eliminate "too big to fail"—nor can that be accomplished without risking severe consequences to the financial system and economy. In fact, the Administration's proposal, which is the basis for the bill in the House, would extend the Federal safety net to nonbank financial companies—a very dangerous idea.

The panic of 2008 was not created by resolving firms like Bear Stearns in a nondisruptive manner. The panic was caused by the schizophrenic manner in which the government handled various troubled firms, bailing out creditors and even shareholders and then giving big haircuts in the next transaction and back and forth. This behavior rattled and confused the markets and created fear that no one was in charge with a coherent plan to contain the damage. The system appeared to be spinning out of control. The final straw was letting Lehman Brothers go down.

The truth is we cannot purge "too big to fail." No major government in modern times has allowed its largest financial institutions to collapse, as it would inflict enormous pain on the entire country or even the world. The FDIC and the Fed must have the authority and means to prevent financial panics, and to deny them that authority would be foolhardy.

It is important to understand what I mean by "too big to fail." It does not mean that shareholders or management of companies should be protected from their mistakes. When the FDIC rescued First Pennsylvania Bank in 1980, it protected the bank and its management and shareholders. I was opposed to that transaction at the time and still believe it was inappropriate. When the FDIC handled the failure of Continental Illinois in 1984, we got it right. Most of the directors were removed, as was senior management, and the shareholders lost everything. Moreover, the FDIC ordered Continental Illinois to shrink its balance sheet by 50 percent over the three-year period following the resolution of the bank.

But the FDIC and Fed went to great lengths to protect and reassure all creditors of Continental Illinois so as not to trigger a conflagration that would spread across the world's financial system.

Restore Glass–Steagall

We cannot allow our largest financial firms to go under in an uncontrolled manner. We can and should implement reforms to make it much less likely that they will fail. One reform Congress should consider is restoring the basic elements of the Depression-era Glass–Steagall Act, which separated investment banking from commercial banking. Investment banking involves very high-risk, high-reward trading and underwriting activities that do not mix well with commercial and retail lending activities funded primarily by conservative bank depositors. Traditionally, investment banks maintained higher capital ratios than commercial banks because the investment banks took higher risks, had more volatile funding sources, and unlike commercial banks did not have access to the federal safety net provided by the Federal Reserve and FDIC.

Various aspects of the Glass–Steagall Act had been liberalized over the years, something I supported and continue to support. For example, banks were given the authority to underwrite revenue bonds issued by state and local governments. Finally, Congress repealed Glass–Steagall in 1999, believing it had outlived its usefulness. I was among those who believed it should be repealed, as I thought regulators could contain the risks and potential abuses.

I believe our experiment with Glass–Steagall repeal has not been successful. We have witnessed a dramatic increase in concentration within the financial services sector and the creation of firms "too complex to manage and regulate." Moreover, investment banks were allowed to leverage themselves beyond the level we would have considered appropriate for the less risky commercial banks.

Paul Volcker opposed repeal of Glass-Steagall and I believe he had it right. He made big news in January 2010 when he stood beside President Obama as the president announced his support for the "Volcker Rule," which would provide that no financial institution may engage in both deposit taking and proprietary trading activities. While this does not go so far as to restore Glass-Steagall, it represents a significant step in that direction, and I strongly support it.

Consolidate and Strengthen Bank Supervision

We must consolidate and strengthen bank and thrift supervision if we are to reduce the chances of future crises. There are state-chartered banks and thrifts and federally chartered banks and thrifts and there are holding companies that own banks and thrifts. State banks and thrifts are regulated by the various state banking departments and by either the FDIC or the Fed at the federal level. National banks are regulated by the Comptroller of the Currency. Bank holding companies are regulated by the Fed, and thrift holding companies are regulated by the Office of Thrift Supervision. The FDIC has a watchdog role over them all.

We must streamline and strengthen this system. The Obama Administration has proposed that the OTS be merged into the Office of the Comptroller of the Currency, its sister agency at Treasury. This strikes me as the equivalent of moving a deck chair on the *Titanic* a foot or two.

Congress should merge the bank, thrift, and holding company supervisory staffs of the Fed, the Comptroller, and the OTS into an independent Financial Institutions Regulatory Authority (FIRA) which would oversee all federal banks and thrifts and their holding companies. The FDIC would remain an independent watchdog over the FIRA institutions as well as state-chartered banks, thrifts, and their holding companies.

This structure will accomplish several very positive things. First, it will consolidate supervision of bank holding companies and their bank and nonbank subsidiaries so that a single agency is looking at the whole enterprise, which will be a vast improvement. Second, it will put bank, thrift, and holding company supervision in an independent agency free of excessive political pressures. Third, FIRA would have two independent watchdogs looking over its shoulder—the Systemic Risk Council and the FDIC. Treasury and Federal Reserve could each have a seat on the board of the FIRA to ensure there is good coordination and information sharing.

Increase Capital, Reserve, and Liquidity Requirements

Stronger buffers are needed to make it less likely that our largest banks will come to the brink of failure. I have been in and around bank regulation for 40 years and have witnessed a continuous battle during that entire period over large bank capital requirements. The largest banks had tangible equity to total assets hovering in the 3 percent range when I arrived at the FDIC in 1978. We fought hard to get that ratio up to the 5 percent range.

During the two decades after I left the FDIC, the Fed and Treasury pushed hard for uniform capital requirements for large banks around the world. They argued that U.S. banks were at a competitive disadvantage vis-à-vis their foreign counterparts because U.S. banks were required to maintain higher capital ratios. The result was the Basel capital accords (Basel I and II), which the FDIC fought every step of the way.

I testified before the Senate Banking Committee at least three times during the past 10 years against the Basel II capital accord. The Basel II accord is a mistake. It uses backward-looking, procyclical models to establish the required capital levels. And it shifts the focus from tangible equity capital to concepts that include subordinated debt and convertible preferred stock. Tangible equity at some of the major U.S. banks declined to the 3 percent range, something bank regulators came to regret in 2008 and 2009.

It is past time to institute the absolute capital standards we all know are needed. This is not a small-bank problem and is not even a medium-size bank problem, as they generally maintain sufficient capital. The largest banks should be required to increase their tangible equity capital ratios, their normalized loan loss reserves, and their normalized liquidity requirements over time. I say "over time" because if we impose higher requirements too rapidly we will impede the ability of banks to lend during the economic downturn.

Eliminate Procyclical Rules

Effective bank supervision is always countercyclical and good bank regulators always lean against the prevailing wind. When everything is bright and sunny without a cloud in the sky, bank regulators should be pushing banks to keep their capital ratios up, build their loan loss reserves, and exercise more caution in the credit granting process. When we are in the middle of a storm, bank regulators should encourage banks without serious problems to increase their lending and work with good borrowers who are having difficulty meeting the terms of their loans.

We have gotten all of this upside down over the past two decades. The SEC and FASB implemented highly procyclical mark-to-market accounting rules that inflate earnings and capital in good times and senselessly destroy earnings and capital when the markets head south. The SEC made it very difficult for banks to build loan loss reserves in good times, which is when they need to be built. Bank regulators implemented the highly procyclical Basel capital accords. Congress enacted legislation allowing banks to avoid FDIC premiums during good times when the fund is flush and forcing them to pay extra assessments during difficult periods. Congress restricted the ability of regulators to use judgment in dealing with troubled banks by putting in place statutory Prompt Corrective Action rules that mandate regulatory enforcement actions.

We must revisit and correct these rules, regulations, and laws. Some of the changes will require congressional action, but much can be accomplished through regulatory action.

Strengthen the SEC and Oversee FASB

The SEC and FASB are the two regulatory organizations that failed us the most leading up to and during the financial crisis of 2008—with Treasury not far behind. The SEC promoted mark-to-market accounting, limited the ability of banks to increase their loan loss reserves during good times, allowed investment banks to triple and even quadruple their leverage at the height of the boom, removed the Depression-era restraints on short sellers just as the boom was ending, and did a miserable job policing investment scams such as the Ponzi scheme run by Bernard Madoff. Even worse, when these failures were brought to the SEC's attention during the buildup to the Senseless Panic of 2008, the SEC sat on its hands and did nothing to remedy the problems it created.

The SEC is broken and badly needs repair and strengthening. One of my disappointments with the Obama Administration and with Congress is that I do not sense that fixing the SEC is a priority. The SEC has always viewed its mission as being to ensure the markets work properly. In the SEC's view, if the markets are provided the right information, they will police and punish inappropriate behavior and risk taking. At the very least, the SEC's mission should be redefined to emphasize its responsibility to become an effective, hands-on regulator of the firms under its jurisdiction.

The FASB is a disaster. We have five unelected and pretty much anonymous accounting lords who meet several times a year in Norwalk, Connecticut, to issue pronouncements on accounting rules that have profound effects on our financial system and economy. Their rules can lead to hundreds of billions of dollars of taxpayer bailouts, foreclosure on millions of homes, the loss of millions of jobs, and the destruction of life savings. Yet no one controls them—they are accountable to no one.

The Defense Department is accountable for its mistakes, the Fed is accountable, the FDIC is accountable, but not the FASB. The SEC is supposed to oversee FASB, but its oversight of the FASB is at least as bad as its oversight of Madoff.

The solution is quite simple. The FASB should be accountable to the Systemic Risk Council the same way the Fed, the FDIC, the SEC, and all the other financial agencies will be accountable.

The lords of FASB do not want to be accountable. I get that—I, too, would like to do whatever I want without oversight or consequence. But that is not the way the world works for everybody but FASB. The FASB needs to be overseen by someone in government and needs to be held accountable for its mistakes. The SEC has proven incapable of performing that oversight function, so it should be given to the Systemic Risk Council.

Strengthen the FDIC

One of the principal watchdogs over the banking system—the FDIC—needs to be strengthened in two ways. The first is to restructure its board. The five-member board consists of three appointed members and two ex officio members (the Comptroller of the Currency and the head of the OTS). When there is a vacancy on the FDIC board, the two ex officio members can deadlock it. When there are two vacancies, the ex officio members are in control of the FDIC. It is untenable that the watchdog agency can be controlled by the heads of two agencies whose banks the FDIC is charged with overseeing.

This is not a hypothetical problem. In 1993, the Comptroller of the Currency and acting director of the OTS were in control of the FDIC board, which had an acting chairman and two vacancies at the time. They presented and adopted a resolution that effectively ended a program I put in place a decade earlier to allow FDIC examiners to accompany the exam teams from the Comptroller of the Currency and the Fed into any bank the FDIC determined warranted closer scrutiny. Because of one or more vacancies on the FDIC board for over a decade, this resolution was not overturned until 2004. The FDIC's congressionally granted oversight authority with respect to national banks, Fed member banks, and thrifts was gutted during the high growth years in banking from 1993 to 2004.

The FDIC board either should not have any ex officio members or they should be nonvoting members. If the Federal Reserve is no longer involved in bank or holding company supervision, I believe it would probably be a good idea to have the Fed represented on the FDIC's board.

The other critical reform is to restore the FDIC's ability to declare that "severe financial conditions" exist so that it can invoke its emergency powers. The FDIC took orders from the Fed and Treasury for most of its existence. It implemented the inappropriately structured bailout of First Pennsylvania Bank on the orders of the Fed and Treasury. The FDIC declared its independence during the handling of the Penn Square Bank failure in 1982. That independence was extremely important during the resolution of the banking and S&L crises of the 1980s.

The FDIC never acted impulsively without coordinating with the Fed and even with Treasury when the stakes were particularly high. But the FDIC did not have to ask, "Mother, may I?" when dealing with the Fed and Treasury, so it was a full partner in the deliberations about how to resolve significant problems.

The panic of 2008 should not have happened. It was poorly handled primarily by the Treasury department, which is not experienced in bank supervision and bank crisis management. It should never again be given such unfettered power and control over the management of crises in the financial system. The Federal Reserve and FDIC should be our go-to agencies in times of financial crisis. Just as generals should fight wars, the seasoned professionals at the central bank and deposit insurer should handle crises in the financial system—there is no room for politicians on either battlefield.

Resolution Authority

We have a safety net (maintained by the Federal Reserve and Federal Deposit Insurance Corporation) and an extensive regulatory regime wrapped around depository institutions. But over the past quarter century, much of our financial system moved from regulated banks and thrifts into a relatively unregulated "shadow" banking system. Bankruptcies and bailouts were tried for these large nonbank firms during 2008, and both were found severely lacking.

The collapse of the credit markets after the Lehman Brothers bankruptcy filing in 2008 illustrates the painful trade-offs. Derivatives' counterparties were able to extract valuable collateral from the firm, and its best assets were sold within days of bankruptcy without benefit of competitive bidding. Credit markets froze as collateral was dumped, and counterparties rushed to rehedge. The Lehman bankruptcy reportedly has cost more than $500 million in fees to attorneys and advisors. Thousands of creditors still wait in line in 2010, as billions in assets remain in limbo. The bailouts of AIG and other large financial entities preserved systemic stability and maintained counterparty relationships, but at significant taxpayer expense.

The largest financial firms are highly interconnected, and they are central to credit and liquidity. The current court-based bankruptcy process ties up those intermediation functions, leads to dumping of collateral onto already stressed markets, and creates uncertainty that freezes the markets. We need a process that recognizes the public interest, provides for financial continuity, and hits those responsible with losses, as the government undertakes an orderly transfer or unwinding of the firms' positions.

We have an effective process for handling the failures of FDIC insured banks, which has been successfully used thousands of times. We take over the banks and sell them in a competitive bidding process. We have even stabilized a very large bank—Continental Illinois in 1984—and then wound it down to a fraction of its size before selling it off, with shareholders losing their entire investment. We should build on this tried and true model to create consistency between banks and nonbanks, as well as between large and small institutions, and eliminate the risk of a disorderly collapse, while making the responsible parties incur losses.

Congress is considering legislation to create an FDIC-style resolution process that, with appropriate safeguards, could be used to resolve the failures of nonbank financial behemoths. Bankruptcy lawyers and others have argued that any new resolution authority would constitute a permanent bailout authority and that we should rely on bankruptcy. I share this concern, particularly in the context of the legislation passed by the House in 2009, but believe it can be squarely addressed in the final legislation.

First, the legislation should not permit assistance to keep a failed institution open indefinitely. Second, bankruptcy should remain the first option, but we should also have an alternative FDIC-style mechanism in an emergency to provide an orderly wind down and avoid a sudden collapse that could hurt all Americans. Third, any proposal should set a high bar to trigger this emergency process. Finally, the legislation must ensure that shareholders and other responsible parties take losses to protect taxpayers and minimize moral hazards.

Afterword

We cannot solve problems with the same thinking we used when we created them.

—Albert Einstein

Shortly after the first printing of this book, Congress enacted and President Obama signed regulatory reform legislation, a 2,300-page bill that will lead to some 10,000 pages of new burdens on our financial system. The legislation would not have prevented the latest crisis and will not prevent the next one. It adds enormous costs and uncertainties at a time when we need to get our banks lending again.

Our government and major financial institutions have violated our trust. Mopping up the economic damage—a glut of foreclosed properties, millions of lost jobs, hundreds of billions of dollars of lost savings—will take time. Restoring trust between the government and the governed and between the captains of industry and the people who invest in their companies and buy their goods and services will be more challenging.

177

Many breakdowns led to the recent crisis: reckless growth of Fannie Mae and Freddie Mac; failure of the government to deal with the real estate bubble; excessive high-risk growth in financial institutions; unwise, highly procyclical regulatory and accounting policies; a politicized and fragmented financial regulatory system; rating agencies pursuing short-term profits at the expense of long-term excellence; and excessive borrowing and spending in the public and private sectors. None of these issues is addressed seriously in the reform legislation.

Once the crisis took hold, the government careened from one troubled firm to the next with inconsistent ad hoc solutions that created the sense that no one was in charge with a coherent strategy. The uncertainty was too much for the markets to bear. They could not determine which firms would topple next or how the government would handle the failures. Market participants lost faith in the government and each other, causing banks around the world to stop lending—even to each other.

In September 2008 the government we had trusted to protect us from panics itself panicked. The Treasury Department threw together the Troubled Asset Relief Program (TARP) plan to purchase $700 billion of toxic assets from financial institutions. The plan was sold to Congress using highly inflammatory language ("financial Armageddon!"), which scared the public even more and deepened the economic downturn.

Treasury lost faith in its own plan and abandoned it almost immediately. Instead of purchasing toxic assets, it invested TARP funds in large financial institutions whether or not needed or wanted. To add insult to injury, Treasury also invested TARP funds in General Motors and Chrysler and their finance company arms.

Government policy remains heavily focused on Wall Street and large institutions. The ill-considered, publicly announced stress test applied to the 19 largest TARP banks so rattled the markets that the government was forced to declare all 19 "too big to fail." Smaller banks, which are deemed "too small to save," drop like flies and no one in Washington cares.

The financial reform legislation adds to the widespread feeling that the system is rigged. The fact that politicians repeatedly make false claims about the legislation fuels the public's cynicism. They say it ends the "too big to fail" problem while leaving in place a dysfunctional regulatory system overseeing five major banks that control over half of the banking system and cannot be allowed to fail without causing economic chaos.

They brag about the new watchdog—the Financial Stability Oversight Council—created to identify and control developing systemic risks. They fail to mention that the Council will be staffed and run by the very agencies that led us into the crisis.

The damage to our institutions will be very difficult to repair. People have lost faith in the American dream—get an education, work hard, save and invest, and build a better life for our children and their children. We trusted that the system would be fair and just for those who played by the rules.

For all of our problems, there is nothing wrong with the United States that we cannot fix if we have the political will and leadership to do it. We need to elect people we can trust to put the government's fiscal house in order and bring proper regulation to the financial sector, both of which are critical to getting the economy going again and restoring our faith in government and the American dream.

Epilogue

I had the distinct pleasure in late 2011 to interview Richard Kovacevich, former Wells Fargo chairman and chief executive officer. Wells Fargo famously navigated the financial crisis better than most of its peers and, indeed, acquired the deeply troubled Wachovia Bank at the height of the crisis without government assistance.

In this interview, which I conducted for *FTI Journal*, the man who led Wells Fargo through the crisis challenges conventional wisdom about what drove the financial catastrophe and suggests a preventive model for the future. Kovacevich also brings his experience to bear on how government actions fueled unnecessary panic and what is needed to emerge from the crisis and spur economic growth.

Dick Kovacevich and I have been friends for about 30 years. He is one of the few executives to have successfully led a major banking company through several economic cycles. You will see in this interview that he is smart, articulate, passionate, and incredibly candid. His perspective—from the inside of a major bank during

180

the crisis—is an important addition to this book. You will also see that we do not always agree, which is also valuable.

William Isaac: Thank you so much for agreeing to do this interview. I'm looking forward to it. You're from the state of Washington, earned undergraduate and graduate degrees from Stanford, and then joined General Mills in planning and marketing. Do I have all that right?

Richard Kovacevich: Yes. I eventually was put in charge of one of the toy companies General Mills owned.

Isaac: I had no idea General Mills was in the toy business. I associate it with food products. At any rate, you then moved to Citibank in the late 1970s and were in charge, at various times, of each of Citi's retail banking businesses. You and I first met in 1982 or 1983 when I was head of the Federal Deposit Insurance Corporation (FDIC). You and a group of other bankers met in my conference room to discuss deposit interest rate deregulation. You must have been quite a character even then, because I have little memory of that meeting or who attended, but I have a distinct memory of you and even where you sat at the conference table.

After a number of years at Citi you went to the former Norwest Bancorp in Minneapolis to become the chief operating officer.

Kovacevich: And we did succeed in abolishing Regulation Q. Yes, I joined Norwest in 1986 as chief operating officer and became CEO in 1993. I became CEO of Wells Fargo when we merged the two companies in 1998.

The Real Risk in Banks

Isaac: At Wells Fargo you created an unparalleled marketing machine focused on growth by increasing the cross-selling of multiple products to existing customers instead of simply making loans and accepting new customer deposits.

Kovacevich: I quickly learned that the riskiest part of the banking business is lending. If a bank's growth is focused on making more loans and its loan risks become concentrated, whether geographically, by borrower, or by industry, the bank's total risk becomes excessive, even if the bank underwrites those loans well. Banks fail due to concentrated risk. By the way, you and I don't disagree on much but we do disagree on the riskiness of big banks. Risk has little to do with the size of the bank . . . in fact, more small banks fail than big banks because they are generally more concentrated geographically, by product, and by industry. Now, if a big bank is concentrated, then obviously it is a higher risk.

Even if you underwrite well, if real estate goes to hell or the economy slows significantly, you're going to get hammered. So you must underwrite well, but then, to mitigate the macro factors you can't control, you have to spread the risk. Risk management in banking should be more like it is in an insurance company. You spread and diversify the risk.

Isaac: I'm not sure why you said that we disagree on that because we actually . . .

Kovacevich: Because you're always writing that the five largest banks control too much of the banking system and that Wells Fargo and the others are so big that they are risky. I believe that the chance of Wells Fargo's failing today at $1.2 trillion in assets is less likely than when I joined Norwest, which was a $20 billion company with a narrow product line concentrated in the upper Midwest and in agricultural-related lending.

Isaac: I don't believe I've ever called for large banks to be broken up. I've called for them to be regulated more intelligently and vigorously because the risks to the system are catastrophic when megabanks get into big trouble. I have argued that megabanks should not be given preferential treatment on capital requirements compared to smaller banks. And I have argued we should have at least debated whether the wall separating commercial from investment banking should be reconstructed in some form. But I'm pretty sure I have never called for breaking up the big banks. We need big banks.

I've noted that the five largest institutions control more than 50 percent of the financial system, and that is an undue concentration. Do you agree with that?

Kovacevich: I don't. Five or fewer companies control more than 50 percent in every industry, from cereal to automobiles. Five banks control more than 50 percent of their industry in about every country in the world.

Isaac: You don't believe banking is different or special compared to, say, the beer or cereal industry?

Kovacevich: No. In any given product line or geography the largest bank has, on average, 15 percent of the business. Some banks are big only because they have product and geographic diversity. That reduces the concentration of risk. If U.S. banks had been allowed to bank nationally from the get-go, as was the case in most other countries, few would even question their market share today. Texas banks in the 1990s were small by today's standards. But they all failed because they were not allowed to bank outside of Texas. Savings and loans in the 1980s, individually, were not big. But they were excessively concentrated and required hundreds of billions of dollars of taxpayer money to be resolved. In the recent crisis, the taxpayer is unlikely to pay a dime for bank failures.

Isaac: I agree that diversification of risk is critically important both . . .

Kovacevich: When we acquired Wachovia, it doubled our size but reduced our risk, because it doubled the geography in which we operate. I believe that deal reduced risk for the system as it increased our ability to serve more customers, with more products and in more geographies, and is absolutely positive for the economy. In short, if a bank becomes big because it has grown to be more diversified in products, geography, and risk, that is a good thing. If it is big because it is even more concentrated, that is a bad thing.

Isaac: What I have also said every time I've addressed the issue is that Wells Fargo, to me, is a large community bank.

Kovacevich: It is.

Isaac: You don't have at Wells Fargo a lot of highly complex and risky activities that some of the other major banks have.

Kovacevich: That's why I get back to concentration of risk. I'm saying that size has little to do with it other than if you are both large and have concentrated risks. That is a very dangerous combination. We must stop focusing on size, per se, and determine whether these firms are diversifying their risks properly. The Dodd-Frank law and the regulators are punishing some banks simply because they are large. It's not right. But anyway, I will get off my soapbox.

Isaac: Let's stay on this a little bit because I think we're into something very important. I agree 100 percent that diversification of risk is critical to the banking industry. I was at First Kentucky before I went to the FDIC. It was the largest bank in Kentucky at that time, and it had 40-some consecutive years of earnings and dividend increases, dating back to the Great Depression. I asked the CEO, "How's that possible?" He responded, "We're not smarter than anybody else and we've made every mistake anybody else has made. The difference is we don't make big bets."

Kovacevich: He was absolutely correct!

Isaac: So I've long believed that diversification of risk is critical and I agree with you that geographic expansion is a very important part of risk diversification. We're on the same page on all that. But some large banks are involved in highly risky activities that are not well understood by the banks, their regulators, or the markets. When they make a mistake, particularly if several large banks are involved in the same activities, the risks to the economy and the FDIC can be enormous.

Kovacevich: Oh, but the systemic impact is still there if you split that bank into three banks and each behaves in exactly the same way. Then all three are going to fail at the same time, just like what happened in the subprime mortgage business. Most of the players in the subprime mortgage origination business were small, but all were doing high-risk subprime mortgages (i.e., concentrated risk). Now, I don't think the crisis could have reached the level it did without their co-conspirators, the investment banks. But it did happen. It brought down the entire economy of the United States and started a worldwide recession.

The point I want to make is that if only the large regulated institutions had originated subprime option ARMs [adjustable-rate mortgages], it never would have gotten to the level it did. It was primarily the small institutions that were originating them. The investment banks were marketing them, and Freddie and Fannie were guaranteeing those loans. [Congressman] Barney Frank has stated on many occasions—and that worries me because I don't often agree with Barney Frank—that the regulated institutions were not the cause of the financial crises.

Isaac: Would you agree that when one or two mega institutions get into trouble it threatens the economy and nation?

Kovacevich: No, I disagree with you. The problem is when two or three or four of them get in trouble.

Isaac: But they tend to be doing a lot of the same things, so . . .

Kovacevich: Well, that's what I'm saying . . . concentration of risk. Think about the investment firm Drexel Burnham that failed in the 1990s. No big deal. Continental Illinois failed in 1984. No big deal. We got through it.

Isaac: I thought Continental was a big deal.

Kovacevich: Well, I know. But you handled it well. I mean, the whole point of your recent book is that if we had had adult supervision in Washington, D.C., during the recent crisis, a lot of the turmoil would not have occurred.

The point is that when you have concentration of risk, whether it's in one company, five, ten, or a hundred, it doesn't make any difference. I'm not saying it isn't a big deal. But I would rather deal with one big institution than 15 smaller ones that collectively are much bigger than the one large institution. Again, remember the S&L industry crisis of the 1980s—hundreds of relatively small thrifts cost the taxpayers $150 billion due to concentrated risk.

Isaac: I agree with you completely on diversification of risk being key to success in banking and preventing a catastrophe. But there are two ways to look at the concentration of risk. One way is to look at it in an individual institution, such as Wells Fargo, and making sure the firm is diversified. The other is to look at it from the point of view of the system. If serious mistakes are being made and five firms control 50 or 60 percent of the banking system, it's really difficult to deal with their mistakes.

Have We Solved "Too Big to Fail"?

Isaac: If I could, I would like to move to something that's related to what we're talking about. The other issue that I have with the large firms involves this "too big to fail" concept. First, let me just ask if you believe that we have, through the Dodd-Frank law, ended "too big to fail"?

Kovacevich: Absolutely not. But too big to fail must be stopped. No bank, none whatsoever, should be too big to fail. I worked on this issue with the Minneapolis Fed 20 years ago. Gary Stern [former president of the Federal Reserve Bank of Minneapolis] has been writing books and papers about this for 20 years. It's very simple—the only way we can solve too big to fail is when it's clear that everybody that supplies capital to a failed bank, except insured depositors, is going to take a haircut [absorb losses] in a failure. That includes the failure of a $300 million bank or a $1 trillion bank. Until we force haircuts on all suppliers of capital to failed banks, we will be living with too big to fail.

Administering haircuts requires a huge liquidity fund from the Fed or the FDIC because it could take months to fully wind down the bank and there's not going to be enough liquidity to do that without the government supplying the temporary funding. But they should be able to be wound down at no cost to the insurance fund or taxpayers. The cost will be borne by the debt holders, uninsured depositors, and the common and preferred stockholders. I believe that haircuts will cause those who provide capital to banks to be more disciplined about to whom and how much capital they provide. They will monitor the bank's risk appetite more closely, and restrict additional capital when the risk grows too large and banks become too concentrated. In fact, I believe their self-interested vigilance will be more effective in reducing bank failures than our regulators have been.

The Bailouts Drove Panic

Isaac: What do you think turned the recent crisis into a panic? What event or events led to the panic?

Kovacevich: One of the most critical was the process of bailing out Bear Stearns and then later not bailing out Lehman. The biggest mistake was not, as most people think, failing to bail out Lehman. The mistake was bailing out Bear Stearns and then not bailing out Lehman. The market just said, "We have no idea what's going on. We don't know what's happening next. We are getting out of the market."

And for the Fed and [former Treasury Secretary Henry] Paulson to say, as they have, that they had no authority to bail out Lehman is simply not true. How can they say they had the authority to bail out AIG but they had no authority to bail out Lehman?

Isaac: They have a big microphone.

Kovacevich: That's right. And everyone, including the media, repeats it without questioning it, except you. It's very unfortunate because we may make the same serious mistakes in the future. So in my opinion, we should not have bailed out Bear Stearns, which was much smaller and much less risky than Lehman. It could have been handled more easily.

If that had happened, there was no question in my mind that Dick Fuld [CEO of Lehman] would have said, "Oh-oh, game's up. I'd better sell this thing right away at whatever price I can get." He might have been able to sell it. I'm told it was close many times. And if Lehman could have been sold, then you might not have had the run on the other investment banks.

Isaac: That's interesting. I certainly agree with your assessment in terms of the schizophrenic actions by the government—bail this one out and let this one fail and bail that one out and let this one fail. That totally rattled the markets because they didn't know what was coming next and how it would be handled. I've argued that stabilizing Bear Stearns was appropriate, and then letting Lehman fail was the mistake. You're arguing that they should have let Bear Stearns go and then Lehman would have taken care of itself.

Kovacevich: Because if they bailed out Bear Stearns and also Lehman, everyone would know that every financial institution was going to be bailed out. Then you're back to too big to fail, squared. I think the reason Lehman was allowed to go bankrupt, and I know Hank [Paulson] pretty well, I think he said to himself, "Well, if we rescue Lehman, then we have to do it for everybody. And we don't have enough money, or political will, to bail out everyone."

When they let Lehman go down, and the markets all crashed and liquidity dried up, they then realized the world was coming to an end. They ran to Congress to get the $700 billion to purchase toxic assets under the TARP [Troubled Asset Relief Program]. Then they realized that the $700 billion for assets would not even put a dent in the problem, so they ended up bailing out everybody by supplying capital.

To cover their mistakes, they claimed they had no authority to bail out Lehman and, with a straight face, bailed out AIG a few days later. Chaos occurs when people don't think in terms of what's the next step if we do such and such now.

TARP and More Panic

Isaac: You mentioned TARP and the $700 billion. Were you in favor of TARP?

Kovacevich: I think TARP was one of the greatest economic mistakes ever made in the history of the United States. It was unnecessary. It solidified too big to fail, forever. It absolutely led to further panic and to the demonizing and vilifying of the banking industry by the Obama administration and Congress. It has even caused our citizens to question our entire free enterprise system, the greatest economic system for creating the most wealth for the most people in the history of the world. It led to the Dodd-Frank bill, which does little to solve the next crises but strangles banks with many regulations that will make it much more difficult and expensive for banks to generate capital to fund our nation's economic growth. Rumors even started flying about nationalizing banks, which was supposedly proposed by Larry Summers [an economic adviser to President Obama]. And then you add on the public announcement of stress tests for the major banks, which led to even more turmoil in the markets. You could not have made more mistakes or caused more uncertainty than these actions.

Everyone says TARP and the stress tests worked when neither one of them worked. After their announcement, the overall stock market fell by 40 percent and bank stocks fell by twice that, 80 percent. So can anyone remotely suggest that TARP revived confidence in the system? TARP destroyed confidence in the system and didn't solve anything. What brought the market back from the TARP debacle was that Wells Fargo reported record first quarter 2009 earnings. Other banks also had better than expected earnings, and investors realized the problem wasn't as big as everyone thought it was. That's what worked, along with Congress holding hearings to scold the SEC [Securities and Exchange Commission] and FASB [Financial Accounting Standards Board] on mark-to-market accounting in March of 2009. Then the creators of TARP took the credit for the better performance. If giving $25 billion of capital to a company like Wells Fargo, because it was supposedly at risk of failure—money that we never used and fully paid back with a double-digit return to taxpayers—could magically cause it to have record earnings less than five months later, then we should do that for every company in America.

Isaac: Intervening at Bear Stearns was not something that gave me a problem. I didn't like the way they did it. I believe the Fed should have simply said, "We are going to support Bear Stearns with liquidity through this crisis, along with others who might need it. We're not going to let this crisis get out of control from a liquidity standpoint." If the Fed had said that and backed it up, I believe the crisis would not have spun out of control. It would have required but a tiny fraction of the two or three trillion the Fed ultimately injected to stabilize the economy. They could have made a determination of which firms were insolvent and needed to be dealt with months later after the markets had stabilized and some semblance of normal pricing had returned.

Kovacevich: I agree with that approach plus a very important addition: haircuts for all suppliers of capital to Bear Stearns if there was a capital shortfall after the wind-down. Also, this is very, very important: you can't rescue large, complex firms over a weekend. Let me make a very important but blunt statement. If our regulators are only capable of knowing that a large institution is likely to fail on Friday, but not before that, such that is must be rescued no later than Sunday night, two days later, then we should eliminate regulators altogether and leave buyers and investors on their own. Ineffective regulation is worse than no regulation at all because it gives investors a sense of confidence that a competent organization is monitoring the company so that they don't have to be vigilant themselves. Potential buyers and regulators need time, at least a couple of weeks, to determine how to sell or liquidate a large and complex company. This means we will need a substantial liquidity fund. This is not in Dodd-Frank. In fact, Dodd-Frank will make it more difficult for the Fed and FDIC to provide liquidity to firms in the middle of the next crisis as Congress and the public will likely consider a liquidity fund as another bailout.

The Fed or the FDIC or whomever you want to use needs to provide liquidity to facilitate the orderly winding down of a failed bank. It could take months to sort through the firm, determine values, sell assets, and work out haircuts for creditors. Someone needs to provide the temporary financing for that.

Isaac: I agree. There is little hope for calming markets and imposing haircuts if the Fed and FDIC are prevented from providing liquidity and stabilizing the financial system in a crisis. The first thing that the Fed needed to do in Bear Stearns was what they did: provide $30 billion of liquidity to Bear Stearns or whatever amount was necessary to calm the crisis. Let the crisis calm down and then figure out what's going on at Bear Stearns. Is it insolvent? Or is it just a liquidity problem?

Kovacevich: But who is going to figure that out, though? I question whether the regulators have the expertise or the motivation to do that job properly. They are primarily concerned with not making waves and having to explain to Congress why they failed to regulate those companies properly in the first place. You've got to have people who are in the market every day, and who know what value is in a particular business because they're in that same business. I think you need some interested parties willing to buy these companies or significant parts of them, hopefully more than one interested party, so there's some competition. The Fed could provide the necessary liquidity for this valuation period, however long it is. Creditors, who should be subject to haircuts, could receive some of their money relatively quickly, with the balance coming later, depending on recoveries.

Isaac: Well, let's take an actual example of something that you and I are both familiar with, probably I more than you: the failure of Continental Illinois in 1984. Continental had a massive run and it lost 25 percent of its liabilities in a couple of weeks. The first thing we did was stabilize it. The FDIC stepped in and put some subordinated debt in Continental. The major banks around the country increased their funding to it, and the Fed agreed to continue funding.

And then we took a period of several months to analyze Continental, get proposals from people to acquire it, and decide what to do. In the end, we couldn't find anybody to acquire it, except on terms the FDIC could not accept. So the FDIC put together its own deal to recapitalize Continental and wipe out the shareholders.

Kovacevich: Yes, it was very well done. It is an excellent example. But you see the problem is that the banks refused to lend money to Lehman. I don't know about Bear Stearns. And you can't do it over a weekend.

Isaac: No, you can't do it over a weekend. But you have to insist that the banks come along on these deals. I assure you that some banks had their arms twisted a bit at Continental.

Revamping the Regulatory System

Kovacevich: So why didn't the arm-twisting work with Lehman? Also, when are we going to admit that our regulatory system is not working properly? For example, everyone in the industry knew that Wells Fargo was not originating subprime mortgages using payment option ARMs and other risky features. We could have originated them and sold them off. We lost 4 percent market share, $160 billion in originations, every year for three years. If the largest company in the mortgage business was not doing something, why didn't the regulators investigate why not?

Isaac: If I understand you, you're saying that Wells Fargo was the largest mortgage originator and was not doing option ARMs, negative amortization ARMs, stated income, or no-doc/low-doc mortgages to subprime borrowers, and that should have been a signal to the regulators that nobody should be doing them.

Kovacevich: Well, they should at least figure out why we weren't. I had the opportunity, at various meetings with regulators, to talk about the subprime situation. I called subprime option ARMs "toxic waste."

Isaac: You were calling option ARMs toxic waste in meetings with regulators?

Kovacevich: Yes, to subprime borrowers. There were CEOs of other banks who disagreed with my characterization of these subprime loans, so you had differences of opinion. No regulator took the time to examine why Wells Fargo felt so strongly about the risks of subprime lending and why the others didn't.

I visited the head of one of our regulators in 2006 well before the crisis. I don't know how we got on the subject, but he asked me what I thought of subprime mortgages. I said, "We are not making subprime option ARM mortgages because we consider them toxic waste." So he said to me, "So you're not doing that?" And I said, "No." He then said, "Well, you're going to lose market share, aren't you?" I said, "Yeah." And I added, "If we're right about it, we will be glad we did because most of the borrowers aren't capable of repaying their loans!"

Now if you have the head of a major bank, whatever you may think of him, you know he wants to make money. You know that he knows the business because his bank is the leader in the industry. And he says, in English—as you know, I do speak very forthrightly—that these loans are toxic waste, and still the regulators didn't do anything about it.

Isaac: How would you change the regulatory system? Is there a way to change the system to make it work better? I've been through three major banking crises in my professional career. How do we keep the cycle from repeating every 10 years or so?

Kovacevich: It gets back to putting the capital providers at risk who may be capable of understanding these complex organizations. First, you have got to impose haircuts on the providers of capital to the institutions should they fail. Second, you have to worry about concentrations of risk, even if the underwriting of risk seems sound. That's what we have been talking about. I don't care how good your underwriting is. You can't allow big concentrations of risk. Finally, why do you punish 8,000 banks with

Dodd–Frank regulation when only about two dozen of them sinned and most of them weren't even banks at the time? You need to severely punish the guilty and reward those who did the right thing even while giving up short-term profits.

Isaac: Because you are inevitably going to make mistakes.

Kovacevich: You do make mistakes or, even more likely, some macro event hits you. In this crisis, we were so smart we didn't do subprime lending. But we were so dumb that we didn't understand or think about that if subprime becomes a massive problem, it would also hit the prime side, where we ultimately lost tens of billions of dollars. We knew home prices were going up somewhat because of subprime. But we didn't connect the dots to see it was also causing the prime homes to go up considerably. Our prime second mortgages, for example, might get hammered, which they did. We also made some underwriting errors in prime second mortgages, especially those originated by outside brokers that we never should have made.

The Mistake of Mark-to-Market Accounting

Isaac: Let's talk about mark to market [MTM], because you and I are probably the two people in the world who hate mark-to-market accounting the most.

Kovacevich: I sure do.

Isaac: What role did it play in the crisis?

Kovacevich: A huge role. People thought the world was coming to an end because everyone was reporting huge book [losses] but not actual losses because of MTM accounting.

I shared with you, during the crisis, an example of where we had to write off $900 million on a prime mortgage portfolio that we thought had a maximum loss exposure of $100 million. Our current loss estimate for that portfolio is now just $35 million. But we had to report nearly a billion-dollar loss that never came to fruition. And that was just one relatively small portfolio. I could give you many more examples.

Also, we wanted to purchase some classes of assets because we knew they were undervalued. They were marked to incredibly low market prices. We were very reluctant to be a purchaser, however, because we'd have to take an MTM loss if the asset went down further even though we knew over the cycle it would be profitable.

Isaac: So let's say that some financial asset had been marked down from 100 cents on the dollar to 60 cents and you were convinced that it was a great buy at 60 cents. You couldn't afford to take the risk because the market might move to 40 before going back up to 90. And you couldn't afford to take the risk of a further 20-cent write-down required by mark-to-market accounting.

Kovacevich: Precisely. Unless it got to some point that we could be highly comfortable was rock bottom. This caused the markets to cease functioning. It destroyed a lot of companies, and ultimately forced the Fed to intervene with trillions of dollars and be the buyer of last resort. Mark-to-market accounting was a huge culprit in the financial crisis and caused unnecessarily massive damage to the economy, and to housing in particular.

Isaac: I gather you share my view that this crisis could've been quite manageable had there not been mark-to-market accounting.

Kovacevich: I don't know if you remember, but I sent you a speech of all kinds of mistakes that let this crisis get out of control. Mark to market is just one. This crisis could never have gotten to the level it did if the rating agencies hadn't rated this stuff triple A. It never would have gotten to this level if the SEC had forbidden the high leverage and inadequate liquidity plans of investment banks. It couldn't have gotten to this level if 71 percent of all the subprime mortgages weren't guaranteed by Fannie and Freddie. For how many decades have we been telling Congress that Freddie and Fannie were accidents waiting to happen? It couldn't have gotten to this point if state regulators had done their jobs with state mortgage brokers who committed outright fraud. It couldn't have got to this level if bank regulators, especially the Office of Thrift Supervision, had been properly examining the banks under their supervision. All of our safety valves failed. I don't think that's ever happened before.

Why Wells Fargo Had to Take TARP Funds

Isaac: Wells Fargo, of course, took $25 billion of TARP funds. I know from our conversations that . . .

Kovacevich: We were forced to take $25 billion over my dead body.

Isaac: That's what I wanted to bring out because I know that you were adamantly opposed to it and spoke out forcefully at the meeting in which you were told you had no choice. I've been told by another participant in that meeting that the banks were told that they didn't have to take the money. "But if you don't take it"—this is Secretary Paulson speaking, I'm told—"you will be visited by regulators next week. They will come up with a capital requirement for your bank that you will find impossible to meet. You'll be back on your knees and begging me to let you have this money. And the terms are going to be a lot tougher."

Kovacevich: That's correct. In fact, it was worse than that for me. When I said, "I don't want your money," Paulson responded, "Your regulator is sitting right next to me who will declare your bank 'capital deficient'." Now, why do you think he used the term "capital deficient"? What can't you do if you are capital deficient? You can't acquire anybody, right?

Isaac: You can't acquire, for sure.

Kovacevich: This was in October of 2008. We wanted the Fed to approve our acquisition of Wachovia no later than December 31st. What is the probability that the Fed would have expedited its approval level for the only institution that did not do what it wanted you to do?

The truth has not come out in this whole thing, by the way. I argued at this meeting that "If Wells Fargo takes this money"— we were triple A rated at that time—"instead of restoring confidence in the system, it's going to destroy confidence because you will be telling the markets that Wells Fargo is in trouble." If a triple-A-rated bank needs government assistance, then no rating will be believed and the world will come to an end.

Now, what happened? You have the statistics. We suffered through a 40 percent decrease in the Dow Jones average between that October date and March of 2009, and an 80 percent decrease in the bank stock index. And they say TARP worked. They say it restored confidence in the system. An 80 percent drop in stock prices is hardly a show of confidence. It shouldn't have been a surprise to anybody, as it was totally predictable. I did my best to convince the authors of the foolishness of TARP and lost.

More Panic from Stress Tests

Isaac: Well, between TARP and the stress test they almost brought the system down.

Kovacevich: Exactly. And I said the same thing on the stress test.

Isaac: I think on the stress test you said publicly, at the time, that it was "asinine."

Kovacevich: That's not correct. I supported the stress test and said so publicly. We do them internally all the time. What I did say is that preannouncing the stress test was asinine.

Isaac: Right. I don't think either one of us would argue against stress tests. You just don't announce that you're doing a stress test. It created so much uncertainty and speculation that the bank stock index declined by 50 percent in the month after the announcement. Eventually Fed Chairman Bernanke had to declare that 19 stress-tested banks were too big to fail.

Kovacevich: Why would you preannounce, for God's sake, except that you don't really understand markets?

How to Emerge from the Crisis

Isaac: Let's switch gears. I'd like your views about how we got into the fiscal crisis and how we're going to get out of it. Also, what do you think the future looks like for the U.S. economy?

Kovacevich: I think what's missing from all the rhetoric is we will never solve our deficit problem—our social commitments, Medicare, pensions, and whatever—by only cutting expenses and raising taxes. The only way that we solve our long-term fiscal problems is by a combination of expense reductions, taxes, and growth. For every 1 percent annual growth in our GDP above a baseline growth number, if that growth can occur for 20 years, per capita income—per capita, not just per household—will increase by something on the order of 25 percent. It's an extraordinary benefit that can fund much of our social needs.

In addition to a deficit commission, we need a growth commission even more. We should ask some experienced business-oriented people what it will take for the United States to generate GDP growth on the order of 1 percent to 2 percent more than we would otherwise experience. What would it take? What are the conditions and environment to produce more growth?

I believe they would come up with something very close to what the Simpson-Bowles Commission suggested on the tax and spending fronts. For the life of me I don't understand why Simpson-Bowles isn't used as a baseline for consideration and why it was totally ignored by the President and Congress. It's a very good starting point.

Start with a process to cut $3 trillion in expenses over the next 10 years and add around $1 billion in revenue from various sources primarily by eliminating special tax reductions for individuals and corporations. Then cut marginal tax rates on those corporations and individuals to stimulate growth. As part of increasing revenue, I would decrease, permanently, the rate of corporate foreign tax repatriation to 15 percent or half the corporate tax rate, whichever is lower. That would raise revenue by roughly $150 billion immediately and even more in the future.

I believe that if we had put together a package like this, Standard & Poor's wouldn't have downgraded U.S. debt. Almost anybody in the high tax bracket today would agree to give up deductions immediately in exchange for the opportunity, should they be able to grow their income, that it would be taxed at a lower marginal rate. They would take that risk. They are the businesspeople, entrepreneurs, and small business owners who are the engines of growth for the economy.

Isaac: The certainty of a lower rate in exchange for giving up deductions will lead to a fairer tax code and higher growth if it were accompanied by significant reductions in spending, phased in over time. I would think everyone would take that deal.

Kovacevich: That's what I'm saying. I think it works for everybody, including the Tea Party. I know there are a lot of people in Washington who don't believe this, but you do not grow an economy by stimulus packages. You grow an economy by permanently reducing marginal tax rates. And you pay for those reductions in tax rates by eliminating deductions. You have to be a believer in our free enterprise system to understand this. We don't have many of those in Washington.

Cross-Selling to Reduce Risk

Isaac: I promised we would return to the cross-selling model at Wells Fargo. Let's do that now.

Kovacevich: Yes, because it's very important. If you're only a lender, the only way you grow is by making more loans. But as you do that, you are increasing your risk and your concentration.

Isaac: Right.

Kovacevich: So the light goes on. The loan is the hook—that's what customers want the most. So you have to give them the loan, and hopefully some deposits will come in return. You now ask yourself: What other products does that customer buy from financial institutions? And what are the risks of those products? And lo and behold, they buy 14 products—both consumers and businesses—and the majority of those products don't entail credit risk. They might involve operational risk, but it's a different type of risk. So you can grow your company while reducing and diversifying your risk. Understand what I'm saying?

Isaac: Absolutely.

Kovacevich: And you say, "Aha, nirvana—I'm now able to grow a supposedly risk business, and the more I do it, the less my risk is. So I have found the magic bullet." Now, if you do that, three other things that you haven't thought of turn out to be true. The cost of selling an incremental product to an existing customer is about 10 percent of the cost of selling that same product to a new customer. Isn't that kind of intuitive and obvious? You don't open up a new account. You don't advertise. You don't take other risks.

Because the margin is so high, you can actually give some of that margin back to the customer. You can say to the customer, if you bring over your treasury management product, your business or personal insurance, your credit card, your 401(k) or whatever, I'm going to give you a better deal than the competitor who is selling you only one product because of the 10 percent cost versus that 100 percent cost. So you have the Walmart phenomenon. Does Walmart sell more products than most other retailers? Does Walmart price higher or lower than its competition?

Isaac: Lower.

Kovacevich: Does it have less or more profits than its competition?

Isaac: Seems to have more.

Kovacevich: Yes, and it's due to their volumes and distribution economics. You give a better deal to your customers, and thcy want to buy more. You benefit because you're making more profits. You benefit from lower risk, and then finally, you have the phenomenon that the more products that customer has with you, the longer they stay with you. Again, I guess this is intuitive but it wasn't obvious to me until I started doing all this.

Isaac: Well, you reduce your cost of creating new customers if you don't have the turnover, and the customers are probably less price sensitive.

Kovacevich: Exactly. Well, they don't even know the price, right? The reason that they don't move is they don't know what my price is on an individual product. This is a dinner menu, not à la carte. If you do more business with us, you don't get charged for your credit card, you don't get charged service fees, and so on. So it's magic. We reduce cost, increase revenue, make higher profits, have less risk, and the customer gets a better deal. This is a business model for financial services that is far superior to any other one that I am aware of.

Isaac: One of the things I've always admired about you and Norwest/Wells Fargo is that I can think of almost no one—no institution, no bank CEO—who has successfully navigated through at least three major economic cycles.

Kovacevich: Yes, because we grow while reducing risk. So it's not hard to navigate. We're not big in anything. We are probably a better risk manager than most. But the key to our success is that we get bigger in a way that diversifies and reduces risk. Let me ask you, is this easy to do or hard to do?

Isaac: Well, I think it's easier relative to the other approaches because you can sleep better at night.

Kovacevich: No, it's harder, much harder, because you need to manage hundreds of businesses and products. Systems have to be capable of aggregating products and profitability by customer so you know what more to sell them and what better deals you can give them to incent them to give you more business. You need to be geographically dispersed. We have 100 different businesses out there doing some very complex things that are difficult operationally and yet they have to work together as if we are one business from the customer standpoint. And that's why most people don't do it. The bad news is that this is hard to do. But the good news is what? That this is hard to do. Anything that has a huge benefit and is easy to do becomes a commodity. If a business model is superior but hard to do, it makes it less likely competitors follow your strategy. Does anyone not know what Walmart does? What its modus operandi is?

Isaac: I think we're all aware of it.

Kovacevich: Why doesn't everybody copy it? Because it's really hard to do. We've lessened credit risk and interest rate risk and all the other stuff that causes problems. We traded off these risks for operational risks, multiple products, systems integrations, and so on that are that are very difficult and complex. By doing that, the barrier to entry increases substantially. And that turns out to be a benefit in disguise. Walmart is a clear example in another field, as they moved from soft goods to become, in addition, the nation's largest supermarket.

Isaac: This is fascinating stuff. I understand better why you feel size is a good thing in banking if handled correctly. Of course, when things go south in a large institution it creates formidable problems in the economy. This leads me to the Glass–Steagall issue, the separation of commercial banking from investment banking enacted in 1934. This separation was repealed by Congress in 1999. Do you believe this repeal helped lead to the crisis in 2008 and 2009?

Kovacevich: Not at all. In fact, if we had eliminated Glass–Steagall 40 years ago, instead of 15 years ago, this crisis is unlikely to have happened. The biggest problem of this crisis was the nonregulated investment banks that grew to an enormous size and with substantial and concentrated risks under the protection from competition by the Glass–Steagall Act.

And I believe one reason why this particular crisis will not happen again is because there aren't many of these bad guys left. The worst offenders are gone and will never come back. The ones that survived are now regulated by the Fed, and therefore there is less chance that they make these obvious bad decisions of high leverage, liquidity issues, and concentrated risk, that the SEC totally ignored.

Actually this gets back to what I said about cross-selling. Wells Fargo can now do investment banking, such as underwriting debt and equity and doing customer hedges and all the standard investment banking activities. We don't have to originate risky structured products or take proprietary trading risk and so on. We have 95 other businesses to make profits from. There's no way that an investment bank can make attractive returns, in my opinion, with their limited product line and their lack of a deposit base, without taking excessive risks and crossing the line of ethical behavior. That's why we were never in that business, in a major way, prior to the crisis.

Isaac: So you're saying that you believe affirmatively that investment banking and commercial banking need to be mixed together?

Kovacevich: Absolutely, for diversity of risk. And what got us into trouble was they weren't. I'm telling you that as bad as Citicorp was, if we didn't have Bear Stearns, Lehman Brothers, Merrill Lynch, Morgan Stanley, and Goldman Sachs, this crisis would never have reached the level it did. I don't even think Citicorp would have done as much. Citicorp survived this crisis, despite doing almost all of the same things as the investment banks that failed, because it was more diversified, including a deposit base.

The Consequences of the Basel Accords

Isaac: Let me give you another controversial topic, because you're on a roll. Where are you on the Basel capital accords? Do you believe that big banks had become overleveraged leading up to the crisis?

Kovacevich: Oh, absolutely, especially the investment banks.

Isaac: So are you in agreement with what the regulators are doing now on capital?

Kovacevich: No.

Isaac: Where do you disagree?

Kovacevich: I think there's way too much capital being required now for some institutions. More risky institutions may need more, however. The regulators have not only increased the capital requirements on everyone, they are proposing to require an additional capital buffer on institutions they consider systemically important even if they are of low risk. It's ridiculous. You don't need that much capital, and it is slowing economic growth to require it.

But let me say this. When the Fed was proposing Basel II a decade or so ago, which would have allowed the largest banks to reduce their capital, I said, "I don't want to reduce my capital." Now they want us to increase it.

Isaac: I know you were opposed to Basel II, as was I.

Kovacevich: Yes, I said it publicly many times. I said I will keep my Tier 1 equity capital at 7 or 8 percent so don't force me to go to Basel II. I don't want my capital reduced. They said we must do Basel II anyway. In addition, despite our track record of strong underwriting on loans, Basel II also would have required us to make our loan decisions based upon—are you ready for this?—credit rating agency ratings. When I first heard this, I almost fell out of my chair.

Isaac: I remember talking to you when Basel II was under consideration. Basically, your view was that we, meaning Wells Fargo, have better credit systems than the regulators were proposing under Basel II. If you make us go to Basel II, we're going to run duplicate systems because we're going to rely on our own system, not Basel II.

Kovacevich: That's what we did, thank God.

Isaac: So you're making us spend $100 million, or whatever amount it was, to implement Basel II and we're going to ignore it for purposes of managing the bank.

Kovacevich: Exactly. But do you know what happened about 12 months ago, what the Fed came out with?

Isaac: Go ahead.

Kovacevich: They said if you are now making your credit decisions using credit rating agency ratings, you must have internal systems to verify that those ratings are correct—totally reversing themselves, after we spent over $200 million to do something we viewed as useless. Think of the systemic and concentrated risk if all Basel II banks in the world had blindly followed the Fed's mandate to base credit decisions on credit rating agency ratings and, as turned out to be the case, these ratings were significantly wrong as they certainly were for subprime mortgages, for almost all structured products, and for many other products and corporations. If this had been implemented, the subsequent financial crisis would have made the Great Depression look like a soft patch. This is from the world's greatest central bank.

A Single Banking Regulator?

Isaac: Let me ask you if you agree with something that I believe. An important reason our regulatory system has let us down so often in the past 40 years is that it's very fragmented. We have a lot of different regulators running around, doing different things. Dodd–Frank seems to have compounded this problem, not alleviated it. Another is that most of the large banks have moved to national charters. This has weakened the Fed as a regulator and has created a competition among regulators. If a large bank wants to do something and the Fed won't let them, it goes to the Comptroller and vice versa. At the same time, our regulatory system has become increasingly politicized with the Treasury, the White House, and Congress much more involved than is healthy. My sense is that we need fewer, stronger, and more independent regulators than we have today.

Kovacevich: I understand your question and your concerns. Let me tell you something that Walt Wriston [legendary former CEO of Citigroup] told me a long time ago. He believed that the worst thing that could happen to this country is a single banking regulator. Their power would be so great and the pressure on them so great that you might as well nationalize the banks. If you see what the Fed has been doing in the last three or four years, you see the potential problems that Walt suggested. Fewer is better. But one regulator, no.

Isaac: Okay, that's fine. I don't actually advocate one but . . .

Kovacevich: Let me give you another anecdote that is relevant. All of this is public information. The Fed called us after they completed our stress test and said we needed to raise something like $15 billion in additional capital. I was shocked. I said, "How did you get $15 billion?" So they gave us their numbers. They had reduced our earnings forecast. There was very little difference in projected credit losses. In fact, I think they actually had our credit losses a few million less than ours. Things where you would expect there might be differences, such as operating expenses, were no different. Instead they had reduced our revenue forecast by over 30 percent, which was the sole reason they had reduced our earnings forecast. I said, "What?"—just making sure I understood.

Isaac: Something tells me you didn't just say "What?"

Kovacevich: "So you are saying that between May and November, our revenue is going to decline by 30 percent?" "Yes, that's what our model shows." I said, "That's mathematically impossible. I couldn't do it even if I tried. Let me see your model." And they said, "We're not going to show it to you." How's that for transparency in prudential regulation?

I pushed back: "How can I accept needing $15 billion in capital when it is based on a revenue assumption that is mathematically impossible?" "That's it," they said. "You need $15 billion." As we stated in our earnings press releases in subsequent quarters, our actual revenue turned out to be even higher than our own forecast. So the Fed's 30 percent revenue reduction and $15 billion capital raise as a consequence of that was totally and completely wrong.

That's what happens when you have a strong single regulator. I know you love the Fed and think they should be the sole regulator. It's a recipe for disaster . . .

Isaac: Now, Dick. Where do you get all this stuff about me?

Kovacevich: You have said that you believe the Fed should have all these powers. That was Dodd's proposal and you supported it. Bill, you said it a thousand times.

Isaac: Senator Dodd's proposal in November of 2009 was to take all of this out of the Fed and put it into a new independent financial institution regulatory authority. I didn't like everything about the Dodd proposal, but I thought he was on the right track, which was to take supervision out of the Fed and the Treasury and put it into an independent banking commission with a separate FDIC.

Kovacevich: Okay, I agree with you that you said that. But I don't consider it any different whether that one regulator is the Fed or a commission or a regulatory authority of a different name. Remember what I stated earlier about the Fed requiring Basel II banks to use credit rating agency ratings to make their lending decisions. What I am saying is that I'd be scared to death of the power of a single anything.

Isaac: I just think we need a stronger federal regulator than we have.

Kovacevich: I could live with the examiners all being in one agency but I worry about a single agency having all of the rulemaking and examination powers.

Isaac: You have been more than generous with you time, Dick. And your candor is always refreshing. You've always been a forceful advocate for the free-enterprise system, and I hope you will stay in the arena and keep up the fight.

Authors' Notes
on Sources

*S*enseless Panic is a book based largely on the experiences of
William M. Isaac as a high-ranking government official, as
a banking lawyer, as a leading consultant to financial institutions throughout the world, and as a commentator. As such, this
book contains his recollection of events and government actions in
which he was personally and professionally involved over a period
of four decades as well as innumerable conversations he had with
people in and out of government.

In addition, this book relies heavily on information developed
from government and corporate documents generally available to
the public.

Quotations from other sources such as newspaper articles are
typically attributed to the publication in which they appeared,
such as the *Wall Street Journal,* the *New York Times,* the *Washington
Post,* or their web sites. There may be rare instances of an unat-
tributed quotation that appeared in a variety of newspapers or
was broadcast on television or radio.

William M. Isaac
Philip C. Meyer

About the Authors

William M. Isaac was appointed in 1978 by President Jimmy Carter to the board of directors of the Federal Deposit Insurance Corporation and was named chairman of the agency in 1981 following the election of President Ronald Reagan. He served until the end of 1985. Mr. Isaac founded The Secura Group, a leading consulting firm, in 1986. He and his former Secura colleagues were acquired by FTI Consulting in 2011. FTI has some 4,000 professionals with offices in 26 countries, and Mr. Isaac serves as Senior Managing Director and Global Head of Financial Institutions. He was elected Chairman of the Board of Fifth Third Bancorp in 2010. Mr. Isaac is a thought leader in the financial world, speaks before audiences around the globe, appears frequently on various television and radio networks, and writes regularly for a variety of leading publications, including the *Wall Street Journal*, *Forbes*, the *Financial Times*, *American Banker*, the *Washington Times*, the *Washington Post*, and the *New York Times*. He resides in Sarasota,

Florida, with his wife Christine and two children, Lennon and Quinn. He has two children by a previous marriage, David and Stephanie.

Mr. Isaac was assisted in the writing of this book by his colleague, **Philip C. Meyer.** Mr. Meyer is a government affairs consultant who spent most of his career with Golembe Associates, Inc. and The Secura Group, LLC. He is the former editor of the *Banking Policy Report*.

Index